NUTRITION & HEALTH

Vegan Diets

DON NARDO

LUCENT BOOKS
A part of Gale, Cengage Learning

GALE
CENGAGE Learning·

Farmington Hills, Mich • San Francisco • New York • Waterville, Maine
Meriden, Conn • Mason, Ohio • Chicago

© 2014 Gale, Cengage Learning

WCN:01-100-101

LIBRARY OF CONGRESS CATALOGING-IN-PUBLICATION DATA

Nardo, Don, 1947-
  Vegan diets / by Don Nardo.
    pages cm -- (Nutrition and health)
  Includes bibliographical references and index.
  Audience: Ages 9-13.
  ISBN 978-1-4205-1151-2 (hbk.)
  1. Veganism--Juvenile literature. 2. Nutrition--Juvenile literature. I. Title.
  TX392.N35 2014
  613.2'622--dc23
                                                                2013047487

Lucent Books
27500 Drake Rd.
Farmington Hills, MI 48331

ISBN-13: 978-1-4205-1151-2
ISBN-10: 1-4205-1151-3

Printed in the United States of America
1 2 3 4 5 6 7 18 17 16 15 14

TABLE OF CONTENTS

Many people today are often amazed by the amount of nutrition and health information, often contradictory, that can be found in the media. Television, newspapers, and magazines bombard readers with the latest news and recommendations. Television news programs report on recent scientific studies. The healthy living sections of newspapers and magazines offer information and advice. In addition, electronic media such as websites, blogs, and forums post daily nutrition and health news and recommendations.

This constant stream of information can be confusing. The science behind nutrition and health is constantly evolving. Current research often leads to new ideas and insights. Many times, the latest nutrition studies and health recommendations contradict previous studies or traditional health advice. When the media reports these changes without giving context or explanations, consumers become confused. In a survey by the National Health Council, for example, 68 percent of participants agreed that "when reporting medical and health news, the media often contradict themselves, so I don't know what to believe." In addition, the Food Marketing Institute reported that eight out of ten consumers thought it was likely that nutrition and health experts would have a completely different idea about what foods are healthy within five years. With so much contradictory information, people have difficulty deciding how to apply nutrition and health recommendations to their lives. Students find it difficult to find relevant, yet clear and credible information for reports.

Changing recommendations for antioxidant supplements are an example of how confusion can arise. In the 1990s antioxidants such as vitamins C and E and beta-carotene came to the public's attention. Scientists found that people who ate more antioxidant-rich foods had a lower risk of heart disease, cancer, vision loss, and other chronic conditions than those who ate lower amounts. Without waiting for more scientific study, the media and supplement companies quickly spread the word that antioxidants could help fight and prevent disease. They recommended that people take antioxidant supplements and eat fortified foods. When further scientific studies were completed, however, most did not support the initial recommendations. While naturally occurring antioxidants in fruits and vegetables may help prevent a variety of chronic diseases, little scientific evidence proved antioxidant supplements had the same effect. In fact, a study published in the November 2008 *Journal of the American Medical Association* found that supplemental vitamins A and C gave no more heart protection than a placebo. The study's results contradicted the widely publicized recommendation, leading to consumer confusion. This example highlights the importance of context for evaluating nutrition and health news. Understanding a topic's scientific background, interpreting a study's findings, and evaluating news sources are critical skills that help reduce confusion.

Lucent's Nutrition and Health series is designed to help young people sift through the mountain of confusing facts, opinions, and recommendations. Each book contains the most recent up-to-date information, synthesized and written so that students can understand and think critically about nutrition and health issues. Each volume of the series provides a balanced overview of today's hot-button nutrition and health issues while presenting the latest scientific findings and a discussion of issues surrounding the topic. The series provides young people with tools for evaluating conflicting and ever-changing ideas about nutrition and health. Clear narrative peppered with personal anecdotes, fully documented primary and secondary source quotes, informative sidebars, fact boxes, and statistics are all used to help readers understand these topics and how they affect their bodies and their lives. Each volume includes information about changes in trends over time, political controversies, and international perspectives. Full-color photographs and charts enhance all volumes in the series. The Nutrition and Health series is a valuable resource for young people to understand current topics and make informed choices for themselves.

A Decidedly Nonvegan World

"The waiter looked at me with a slightly bewildered expression," Karen, a mother of two in her thirties, recalls. She and two girlfriends had gone out to lunch in a family restaurant in their local mall, and when it was her turn to order she told the waiter she was a vegan. "I could tell by the look on his face that he wasn't quite sure what that word meant," Karen continues.

"Is that like being a vegetarian?" he asked, with a tentative tone of voice. It was clear that he didn't want to sound uninformed. "No," I told him in a friendly way. "Vegetarians don't eat meat. Vegans also don't eat meat, but they stay away from other kinds of animal products, too, like eggs and butter." A sudden look of understanding came over him, sort of like that image you see in old cartoons where a little light-bulb appears above somebody's head. I went on to say that I could see there wasn't anything on the menu that was specifically vegan and asked him if he could bring me a house salad, but without any cheese, another animal-based product that vegans avoid. I also got a side order of steamed broccoli with cranberry vinaigrette, the same dressing I was having on my salad.[1]

A Failure to Provide for Vegans

Karen's successful attempt to order vegan food in a nonvegan restaurant is an incident that is repeated thousands of times each day across the United States, as well as in many other countries. Clearly, most restaurants do not offer vegan dishes on their menus. This is not because they have anything against vegans, but rather for one or both of two main reasons. First, like Karen's waiter, a large number of Americans, including restaurant owners and managers, are at best only vaguely aware of what veganism is and what vegans believe and eat.

Karen tried to remedy that situation in her own small way by educating the waiter, who mistakenly assumed that vegans and vegetarians were the same. She realized it was neither the time nor place for her to go into any more detail about what veganism is or is not. For that, one can turn to the website of any one of dozens of vegan organizations that exist in the United States, Britain, and elsewhere. For example, the American Vegan Society, a nonprofit group that regularly educates people about vegan diet and lifestyle, offers the following straightforward definition:

> Veganism is compassion in action. It is a philosophy, diet, and lifestyle. Veganism is an advanced way of living in accordance with reverence for life, recognizing the rights of all living creatures, and extending to them the compassion, kindness, and justice exemplified in the Golden Rule. Vegans exclude flesh, fish, fowl, dairy products (animal milk, butter, cheese, yogurt, etc.), eggs, honey, animal gelatin, and all other foods of animal origin. Veganism also excludes animal products such as leather, wool, fur, and silk in clothing, upholstery, etc. Vegans usually make efforts to avoid the less-than-obvious animal oils, secretions, etc., in many products such as soaps, cosmetics, toiletries, household goods and other common commodities.[2]

The second major reason that most restaurants do not offer vegan dishes to their customers is that the number of vegans in society is so small that the average restaurant has little or no demand for dishes that vegans prefer. In fact, vegans make up a tiny minority of the populations of most countries. Various surveys have found that in the United

Although it can be challenging for vegans to find restaurants and other businesses that provide vegan options, establishments that cater to the vegan lifestyle are growing in number.

States only about 1 percent, or a bit more than 3 million people, are vegan. (In contrast, these studies found that roughly 3 percent, or between 9 million and 10 million of the total of about 315 million Americans, are vegetarians.)

Thus, Karen's experience at the restaurant highlights a major challenge to vegans in what is largely a decidedly nonvegan country, as well as nonvegan world. A failure to provide for, accommodate, or often even consider the needs and wants of vegans involves more than restaurants. It also extends to a majority of grocery stores, department stores, clothing manufacturers, toy makers and toy stores, hotels and motels, and a wide range of other economic and social institutions.

In addition, many other aspects of modern society do not operate in the way that vegans might prefer. To their disdain, millions of cows, pigs, sheep, fish, and other animals are slaughtered daily to provide food for people's dinner tables. Vegans also oppose water pollution, soil depletion, and other environmental ills that they claim are by-products of raising large numbers of animals for human consumption. Some (though certainly not all) vegans also oppose keeping pets in the home and consider pet ownership a form of involuntary servitude.

An Uphill Battle

Because of their tiny numbers, vegans do not have the political power and influence to make significant changes to such practices. As a result, the average vegan tends to do what little he or she can to maintain and when possible promote vegan diet, values, and lifestyle in a society that frequently views these things as odd and/or extreme. For Karen, teaching her waiter the difference between a vegetarian and a vegan was a small but positive step in what she considered the right direction.

Karen also did what most vegans learn to do when they find themselves in a nonvegan restaurant. Namely, she asked her server to modify an existing item on the menu slightly—in this case by leaving off the cheese. The vegans who oversee the vegan-friendly website EthicalPlanet.com emphasize that very commonsense approach, saying, "Check out the menu, and look for items that are nearly vegan. Don't be too shy to ask if they can be modified to be free of cheese, milk, or whatever the offending ingredient is. Most restaurants are happy to comply with your request."[3]

Meanwhile, some vegans attempt to change social and economic practices they despise by convincing others to make some sort of change. That change might be to switch from a "normal" meat-eating diet to a vegetarian one, or even better, a vegan diet. Or they might persuade one or more people to consider vegan ethical grievances by having frank discussions with friends or friends of friends, through explaining vegan beliefs on Facebook and other social networking platforms, or by writing and/or distributing pamphlets that present vegan views and handing them out in public venues. However even a small effort, vegan author, blogger, and activist Erik Marcus points out, can pay bigger-than-expected dividends later. "It's probable," he says,

> that by investing just thirty minutes in simple outreach, you'll keep as many animals out of factory farms and slaughterhouses as you would by following

a totally vegan diet for the rest of your life. . . . Perhaps the animals' greatest hope is the fact that anyone who cares enough to act, and who contributes either time or money toward simple outreach efforts, can spare millions upon millions of animals from a lifetime of suffering.[4]

Marcus hopes that he will see major progress in the advancement of vegan views in his lifetime. But he is well aware that it will be an uphill battle. He knows that meat eaters largely control and run the world. Indeed, registered dietitian, nutritionist, and practicing vegan Brenda Davis quips, "When animal products are present in everything from gelatin-based camera film to glues, you may wonder if being vegan is possible at all!" She takes heart, however, by looking at the promotion of veganism as a challenge, no matter how hard it might be in a nonvegan world. "Every step you take makes a difference," she tells her fellow vegans. "When you make choices out of love of human life, animal life, or the life of this planet (or all three), you make this world a better place, and there is no greater cause for celebration."[5]

CHAPTER 1

Veganism Through the Ages

No one knows who the first people to eliminate all animal products from their diet were. The identities of these initial vegans, as well as the first vegetarians—those who simply refrained from eating animal flesh—are lost in the distant, muddled mists of time. What does seem quite clear to anthropologists, scientists who study human origins and behavior, is that early members of the human family were omnivores. That is, they consumed both meat and plant products.

This made sense as a strategy for survival in the ages before people discovered agriculture and settled down in permanent villages. As hunter-gatherers moving from place to place, early humans often did not know where their next meal would come from. Searching for enough berries, roots, and other plant products to keep from starving was time-consuming and uncertain. So they learned to supplement an herbivorous diet with meat from rabbits, deer, wild boar, and other beasts when they could get it. The appeal of this approach was that a given amount of animal flesh has a higher caloric content than the same amount of vegetable matter.

When the roving groups of hunter-gatherers finally adopted agriculture, beginning about twelve thousand years ago, they remained omnivorous. They not only grew grains and other crops, but also raised cattle, pigs, sheep, and other animals. From these creatures they obtained both meat and by-products such as eggs, milk, and hides. To get the meat and hides, they had to slaughter the animals, which became a time-honored ritual that farmers taught their children.

At some point, however, anthropologists speculate that one of those children took pity on the creatures in his or her pen or corral. Moved by the animals' suffering, the child decided to stop eating meat, thereby becoming the first vegetarian. When this child or perhaps one of his or her own children or grandchildren went further and gave up milk, hides, and other animal by-products, that anonymous individual had the distinction of being history's first vegan.

The Compassionate King

It is possible that at least a few vegans existed in some or all of the human societies that prospered in the centuries that followed. More certain is that the first known large-scale or society-wide practice of not eating meat occurred in India in the seventh and sixth centuries B.C. Two major religions that began in India in that era—Jainism and Buddhism—promoted the concept of nonviolence toward animals. (That idea may have been considerably older among the precursors of the Jains.)

Treating animals with compassion and avoiding the eating of meat became widespread with the accession of the Buddhist king Ashoka (or Asoka, 304–232 B.C.). Now viewed as one of the greatest rulers in human history, at first Ashoka gave no inkling that he would eventually come to advocate nonviolence toward both people and animals. In fact, he started out like most other ancient national leaders—as an opportunist and conqueror. In 260 B.C. he attacked and overran a neighboring kingdom, killing at least 100,000 people and driving another 150,000 from their homes.

It was during the aftermath of this tremendous massacre that Ashoka had a completely unexpected and unprecedented change of heart. The sight of the immense bloodshed and suffering his soldiers had caused suddenly horrified and sickened him. In that instant he decided he would never shed

In 260 B.C. King Ashoka of India, appalled at the slaughter of war, converted to Buddhism, became a vegan, and outlawed the killing of animals.

blood again, for any reason. Furthermore, he felt it only fitting to share his new philosophy with his subjects. He was "deeply pained by the killing, dying, and deportation that take place when an unconquered country is conquered," he told them in inscriptions carved on rocks and pillars across his realm. "These misfortunes befall all as a result of war," he went on. "Therefore the killing, death or deportation of a hundredth, or even a thousandth part of those who died during the [recent] conquest . . . now pains [me]. Truly, [hereafter] non-injury, restraint, and impartiality to all beings [must be a more moral policy]."[6]

To set an example, the newly compassionate king converted to Buddhism, which advocates nonviolence toward all living things. In another inscription, he called on people to do their utmost to be good and kind and strive always for "generosity, truthfulness, and purity." They should also refrain from "violence, cruelty, anger, pride, and jealousy." Hopefully, he added, this would allow them to achieve "happiness in this world and the next."[7] A major part of a nonviolent approach to living, Ashoka insisted, must be doing whatever was possible to keep animals, no less than humans, from suffering needlessly. This resulted in a ban on slaughtering cattle and other creatures, which radically reduced meat eating in much of India. The king addressed the ban on killing animals in one of his pillar edicts, saying:

> Twenty-six years after my coronation, various animals were declared to be protected—parrots [and] geese, wild ducks . . . bats, queen ants, terrapins, boneless fish, [and] tortoises, porcupines, squirrels, deer, bulls . . . wild asses, wild pigeons [and] all four-footed creatures that are neither useful nor edible. Those nanny goats, ewes and sows which are with young or giving milk to their young are protected, and so are young ones less than six months old. [Also] husks hiding living beings are not to be burnt and forests are not to be burnt either without reason or to kill creatures. One animal is not to be fed to another. . . . During [religious holidays] animals are not to be killed in the elephant reserves or the fish reserves either [and] bulls are not to be castrated [and] horses and bullocks are not be branded.[8]

The Pythagoreans

During the same centuries that vegetarianism and veganism were taking strong hold in India, a few people in faraway Greece and Italy began to adopt that dietary behavior as well. It is possible that this was mere coincidence. But some historians think there may have been some sort of cultural influence at work, perhaps the result of long-distance traders sharing ideas.

The Greeks in question were followers of Pythagoras, a talented mathematician and philosopher, who is famous for suggesting that nature's underlying fabric is composed of complex numerical relationships. A native of the Greek island of Samos, Pythagoras, along with his followers, moved to southern Italy in about 530 B.C. There they established a small religious community and philosophical school. They led a strict, monk-like existence in which they practiced self-denial and renounced meat eating.

The Pythagoreans' ban on meat eating may have been the result of their belief in reincarnation. Thinking the soul to be immortal, they held it could return not only in a person's body, but possibly also in an animal's physical frame. Therefore, if one ate meat, he or she might be consuming a form of a deceased human, and thereby committing cannibalism. In

Pythagoreans were followers of the teachings of Pythagoras, a Greek mathematician and philosopher. They lived a communal life and were vegetarians.

Humans Not Designed to Eat Meat?

The noted ancient Greek biographer and thinker Plutarch was a vegetarian for at least a portion of his adult life and wrote about avoiding meat eating in his great collection of essays, the *Moralia*. In the following passage he argues that human meat eating goes against nature.

> That man is not naturally carnivorous is, in the first place, obvious from the structure of his body. A man's frame is in no way similar to those creatures who were made for flesh-eating. He has no hooked beak or sharp nails or jagged teeth, no strong stomach or warmth of vital fluids able to digest and assimilate a heavy diet of flesh. It is from this very fact, the evenness of our teeth, the smallness of our mouths, the softness of our tongues . . . that Nature disavows our eating of flesh. If you declare that you are naturally designed for such a diet, then first kill for yourself what you want to eat. Do it, however, only through your own resources, unaided by cleaver or cudgel [club] or any kind of axe. Rather, just as wolves and bears and lions themselves slay what they eat, so you are to fell an ox with your fangs or a boar with your jaws, or tear a lamb or hare in bits. Fall upon it and eat it still living, as animals do. But if you wait for what you eat to be dead, if you have qualms about enjoying the flesh while life is still present, why do you continue, contrary to nature, to eat what possesses life?

Plutarch. "On the Eating of Flesh." In *Moralia*, translated by Frank C. Babbit. Cambridge, MA: Harvard University Press, 1957, pp. 551–553.

contrast, the third-century-A.D. Greek biographer Diogenes Laertius recounted a different reason. "Mainly why Pythagoras prohibited a meat diet," he said, "was in order to strengthen his followers' power and will and accustom them to simplicity of life. Furthermore, he wished them to restrict their diet to what was easily procurable, eating uncooked foods and drinking nothing but pure water. Such, he believed, was the way to a healthy body and a keen mind."[9]

Although Pythagoras admonished his friends to avoid meat, it is doubtful he was a true vegan. In this case the evidence suggesting that he did consume some animal by-products comes from the third-century-A.D. Greek thinker Porphyry. Porphyry wrote that Pythagoras drank milk and ate honey and honeycomb, the latter two of which are produced by bees. Bees and other insects, vegans say, are no less animals than are horses and dogs.

Animals Entitled by Birth and Being?

Part of the problem with trying to piece together what Pythagoras and his followers ate and did not eat is that none of their own writings has survived. A non-meat-eating Greek whose literary works *have* survived (at least most of them) was the prolific biographer and moralist Plutarch, who flourished in the first century A.D. In his *Moralia* (*Moral Essays*), he addressed meat eaters, citing unnecessary cruelty to animals and other reasons they should consider giving up animal flesh. "Are you not ashamed to mingle domestic crops with blood and gore?" he began.

> You call serpents and panthers and lions savage, but you yourselves, by your own foul slaughters, leave them no room to outdo you in cruelty. While their slaughter is their [manner of] living, yours is a mere appetizer. It is certainly not lions and wolves that we eat out of self-defense. On the contrary, we ignore these and slaughter harmless, tame creatures without stings or teeth to harm us, creatures that, I swear, Nature appears to have produced for the sake of their beauty and grace. . . . For the sake of a little flesh we deprive them of sun, of light, of the duration of life to which they are entitled by birth and being. Then we go on to assume that when they utter cries and squeaks their speech is inarticulate, that they do not, begging for mercy, entreating, seeking justice, each one of them say, "I do not ask to be spared in case of necessity; only spare me your arrogance! Kill me to eat, but not to please your palate!" Oh, the cruelty of it![10]

It is uncertain whether Plutarch was a vegetarian or what today would be called a vegan. But there is little doubt that vegans existed in the Greco-Roman world. In a large treatise appropriately titled *On Abstinence from Animal Foods*, Porphyry, who did eat meat, mentioned some of the arguments he heard from others who were against meat eating. One of those arguments went:

> One should neither use milk, nor wool, nor sheep, nor honey. For, as you injure a man by taking from him his garments, thus, also, you injure a sheep by shearing it. For the wool which you take from it is its vestment. Milk, likewise, was not produced for you, but for the young of the animal that has it. The bee also collects honey as food for itself, which you, by taking away, administer to your own pleasure.[11]

These ideas are clearly vegan. Porphyry himself disagreed with them, stating that because people took care of many animals, including bees, it was only fair that humans be able to use some of the products produced by those creatures. That sort of vigorous, rational debate over opposing opinions was typical of ancient Greek and Roman thinkers.

Such debate was not seen much or at all in Europe in the medieval centuries following Greco-Roman civilization's fall in the fifth and sixth centuries, however. This was because the Christian Church exercised close control over medieval life and thought. That thought was heavily influenced by Christian thinkers like Saint Augustine and Saint Thomas Aquinas. They felt no particular reverence or concern for the fortunes of nonhuman life, so they had no moral problem with the idea of meat eating. (Some monks and other medieval religious folk did avoid eating meat sometimes. But this was done to deny themselves something they normally enjoyed in order to show submission to God, rather than out of deference to the suffering of animals.) "We look in vain," a nineteenth-century writer said of medieval Europe, "for traces of anything like the humanitarian feeling of Plutarch" for animals. "In those terrible ages of gross ignorance, of superstition, of violence, and of injustice—in which human rights were seldom regarded—it would have been surprising indeed if any sort of regard had been displayed for the nonhuman [living things]."[12]

Growth of a Movement

As the medieval era began to give way to early modern times, however, such regard for animals and the modification of

Italian Renaissance artist and inventor Leonardo da Vinci was one of the earliest known vegans.

one's diet to reflect that concern began to appear again. One of the first notable examples was the great Italian Renaissance artist and inventor Leonardo da Vinci (died 1519). That he abstained from meat eating is clear from one of his more emotional statements. "Truly," he said, "man is the king of beasts, for his brutality exceeds them. We live by the death of others. . . . I have since an early age abjured [rejected] the use of meat, and the time will come when men will look upon the murder of animals as they look upon the murder of man." Various other surviving quotes by Leonardo suggest that he was not merely a vegetarian but also what would later be called a vegan. He criticized human consumption of both milk and eggs, as well as honey, saying that "whole populations" of bees "are destroyed so that we can have their honey." In despair he cried out, "Oh, Justice of God! Why do you not awake and protect your misused creatures?"[13]

In the century following Leonardo's passing, other prominent Europeans began to champion vegetarianism and veganism. In England, for instance, well-known merchant and author Thomas Tryon openly advocated the idea that animals had certain rights and that people should respect those rights by not eating meat. For the most part, however, European philosophers continued to advance the notion that animals had been placed on earth strictly for human use and therefore had no rights.

Such attitudes started to change during the 1700s and early 1800s, when the effects of the Enlightenment began

An Early Vegan Pioneer

One of the early modern pioneers of vegan diets was a brilliant, hardworking nutritionist named William Lambe, who died in 1848. A member of the Royal College of Physicians in London, in 1806 he became concerned about his own health. Hoping to feel better and live longer, he changed his diet and thereafter ate only vegetable foods. At the time, the term *vegetable* denoted all kinds of plants and other things that grew from the ground, so Lambe's diet included grains, fruits, beans, nuts, and so forth. He left behind a number of writings, among them a book titled *Water and Vegetable Diet in Consumption, Scrofula, Cancer, Asthma, and Other Chronic Diseases*, published in 1815. In the book he made the classic vegan statement, "My reason for objecting to every species of matter to be used as food, except the direct produce of the earth . . . is founded on the broad ground that no other matter is suited to the organs of man. This applies then with the same force to eggs, milk, cheese, and fish, as to flesh meat."

Quoted in John Davis. *World Veganism: Past, Present, and Future*. International Vegetarian Union. www.ivu.org/history/Vegan_History.pdf.

to be felt across Europe and North America. Enlightenment thinkers advocated a number of progressive, modern views, including the concept that certain ethical values and rights existed in nature and that human societies should recognize and honor them. Moved by such ideas, English poet Percy Bysshe Shelley, noted physician William Lambe, and several other European artists and intellectuals became vegetarians. In America, meanwhile, founding father Benjamin Franklin did the same. Particularly influential on both sides of the Atlantic was the book *Return to Nature* by English social reformer John Frank Newton, who called for the ethical treatment of animals and the adoption of a meatless diet.

Britain and its former American colonies were not the only lands touched by these ideas. On Europe's eastern flank, the great Russian writer Leo Tolstoy, best known for his epic novel *War and Peace*, became a vegetarian and from time to time wrote about what he saw as its virtues. In his 1892 essay titled "The First Step," he recalled, "Not long ago I had a talk with a retired soldier, a butcher, and he was surprised at my assertion that it was a pity to kill [animals], and said the usual things about its being ordained [by God]. But afterwards he agreed with me [and said] 'Especially when they are quiet, tame cattle. They come, poor things! trusting you. It is very pitiful.'"[14]

Tolstoy was also confident that the vegetarian movement and lifestyle would continue to grow in popularity over time. "The moral progress of humanity, which is the foundation of every other kind of progress, is always slow," he stated.

> But the sign of true, not casual, progress is its constancy and its continual acceleration. And the progress of vegetarianism is of this kind. That progress is expressed in the actual life of mankind, which from many causes is involuntarily passing more and more from carnivorous habits to vegetable food, and is also deliberately following the same path in a movement which shows evident strength, and which is growing larger and larger, as regards vegetarianism. That movement has during the last ten years advanced more and more rapidly. More and more books and periodicals on this subject appear every year. One meets more and more people who have

given up meat; and abroad, especially Germany, England, and America, the number of vegetarian hotels and restaurants increases year by year.[15]

Toward a Brighter Future?

As the number of vegetarians increased in Europe and America, they began to establish formal organizations. The British Vegetarian Society was created in 1847. A few years later it published the highly influential *A Plea for Vegetarianism*, penned by Henry Salt. Most members of the group still drank milk and ate eggs. But over time some of them came to feel that all animal products should be avoided. So in 1944 several members of the society broke away and established the British Vegan Society. This also marked the coining of the term *vegan* to differentiate the members' more restricted diet from traditional vegetarianism.

The first vegan organization in the United States appeared just four years later. In 1960 it blended into a larger group—the American Vegan Society, founded in New Jersey by H. Jay Dinshah. Since that time a number of prominent Americans have become poster children, so to speak, for the vegan movement by converting to a diet that excludes animal products. Among them are boxer Mike Tyson and actor Alec Baldwin. Chelsea Clinton, daughter of President Bill Clinton, is another. In 2010, after her father underwent heart surgery, she convinced him to switch to a vegan diet, which he still maintains.

The future of the vegan movement is difficult to predict. Some people see vegans as oddball characters on society's fringe and assume they will remain a small minority. Vegans are often portrayed as "cranks and amusing wackos," says journalist and vegan Chris Grezo. But he points out that vegetarians were once viewed the same way and today are widely accepted. "Veganism is the new vegetarianism," he states, "and this is why I'm positive about being vegan." Indeed, Grezo and most other vegans think the movement has a bright future. They equate its ultimate

HEALTH FACT

In 1994 vegans around the globe began celebrating World Vegan Day on November 1, the anniversary of the founding of the British Vegan Society.

Some people see vegans as oddball characters on society's fringe and assume they will remain a small minority.

popularity and success with a corresponding improvement in the way animals are treated. The more meat eaters who become vegans, their argument goes, the fewer animals will be mistreated and killed specifically so people can eat them. "It's heartening," he adds, "to see the parallels between the animal rights movement and earlier ethical movements. Over the last hundred years, great gains have been made in the ideological battle for animal rights. The momentum is with us, and though it will be a long journey, it is a journey that has been traveled before, with great success."[16]

CHAPTER 2

Adopting a Vegan Diet and Lifestyle

The fact that vegans have such a long and rich history gives individuals who are contemplating adopting a vegan diet and lifestyle a great deal to reflect on and emulate. Indeed, that history shows in part that there are a number of different reasons for becoming a vegan, and no two people take the exact same route to embracing veganism. Some people choose a vegan diet for health reasons. Others do so because they have strong ethical reservations about how the animals from which meat is derived are treated. Still others are concerned that raising animals to slaughter them for their meat hurts the environment.

There are also vegans who choose their way of life for all of these reasons or for others, including the hope of making a positive contribution to society. According to the Vegetarian Resource Group, a nonprofit organization that educates the public about vegetarianism and veganism, "Many vegans choose this lifestyle to promote a more humane and caring world. They know they are not perfect, but believe they have a responsibility to try to do their best, while not being judgmental of others."[17] In contrast, some vegans *are* openly judgmental of meat eaters and actively criticize the meat and dairy industries, along with people who buy and wear garments made from animal skins, hides, fur, and so forth.

Trying to Define Veganism

There is no single definition for who is vegan or what constitutes a vegan diet. In fact, even vegans themselves frequently disagree over the terminology. Some call themselves "dietary vegans," meaning that they refrain from consuming animal products but may wear clothes made from animal parts. Other terms commonly used to describe this branch of vegetarianism is "flexible vegans," "partial vegans," and "total vegetarians." These individuals often feel they have a right to call themselves vegans even though they still use some animal products. Typical is the case of Alan, a computer programmer in his thirties, who states:

According to the Vegetarian Resource Group, some vegans believe their lifestyle promotes a more humane and caring world.

> I'm mainly a dietary vegan. That means I don't eat any animal products, but I don't carry it into the rest of my life, like in the case of clothes and stuff. You know, I still wear wool and leather. I have a couple of leather

belts and some leather shoes and a leather coat. The way I look at it is that when the animals are already dead, because some people used them for food, you might as well use the bodies to make useful things. Otherwise, it's wasteful, and those animals died for nothing, except to become somebody's next meal. If we use their bodies to make stuff, it's like they didn't die in vain, you know what I mean?[18]

Many vegans argue that there is no such thing as a "dietary vegan." They contend that such a person can call him- or herself a vegan only by adopting a lifestyle that rejects the use of all animal products, including leather and silk.

Many other vegans reject this approach and argue that there is no such thing as a dietary vegan. According to this view, a person can call him- or herself a vegan only by rejecting all animal products, whether those products end up going to waste or not. According to Joanne Stepaniak, a leading authority on veganism:

> Until one's commitment extends beyond the scope of food, the word *vegan* does not apply, regardless of how the media or certain individuals or groups wish to employ it. Unlike vegetarianism, being vegan does not entail simply what a person does or doesn't *eat*— it comprises who a person *is*. People who are vegan attempt to imbue every aspect of their lives with an ethic of compassion. This influences their day-to-day choices and colors their political perspectives, social attitudes, and personal relationships.[19]

Stepaniak and those who agree with her see themselves as the true vegans and feel no need to modify the term *vegan* with other descriptive words, as so-called dietary and flexible vegans do. Yet some of the stricter vegans have no problem with employing modifiers such as *ethical*, *total*, or *abolitionist* to differentiate themselves from people who eat a vegan diet but continue to use other animal products. "'Ethical veganism,' which I use interchangeably with 'abolitionist veganism,'" vegan activist and blogger Gary L. Francione says, "goes beyond a vegan diet and rejects direct animal consumption or use of any kind."[20]

Becoming a Vegan

These marked differences of opinion within the vegan community clearly show that a person who contemplates becoming a vegan may end up defining veganism in his or her own way. Those who call themselves dietary vegans may come to see ethical vegans as too strict. Meanwhile, stricter vegans may continue to insist that those calling themselves dietary vegans are not really vegans.

In spite of such differences, what ties all of these people together are certain shared experiences. Because both dietary and ethical vegans tend to eat the same foods, those experiences usually revolve around food. First, all vegans are drawn to a vegan diet for a reason, which differs from person to person. Often, someone is introduced to a vegan diet through a friend or acquaintance, as in the case of Susan, a single cosmetics supplier in her forties. "The vegan lifestyle was frankly something I knew almost nothing about until a new friend introduced me to it," she says.

> We were out shopping and I noticed a leather coat I particularly liked, and when I asked her what she thought about it she said she didn't use any leather products, which really piqued my interest. She explained that leather is an animal product, which I already knew but had never given much thought. She told me how she was a vegan and that serious vegans don't use any animal products because of the way people get them. . . . At first, I thought this was a bit extreme. But over the course of a few months I came to see the logic of it. I came to see that the animals often suffer and die just so some humans can use their skin or some other part of their body. Now, I'm a strict vegan. I not only don't use any leather products, I also stay away from fur-lined coats and other clothes with fur.[21]

Sometimes nonvegans become vegans when they are in the midst of implementing a new health or exercise program. This was how Cheri, a woman in her forties who works in human services, discovered the vegan diet. "I 'fell' into veganism really," she recalls.

> I was very much into my health and had signed up for an "ultimate body challenge." The diet that went with the workout was very healthy and lean. I was only to have chicken, fish, egg whites, and some cheeses as protein choices. [Over time] I got tired of eating such a limited diet and slowly subtracted each [of these animal products] and found new [plant-based] protein sources.[22]

Quite a few others who adopt vegan diets do so gradually, over the course of a few or even several years. Judy, a sales manager who is married and in her sixties, is one of them. When asked what drew her to veganism, she answered:

> Probably my mother's influence, although she was not vegan. She loved animals, and when I was a child would tell me that the chicken we ate was made in

Surrendering to Buffalo Wings

Surveys reveal that a fairly high percentage of people who try vegetarianism or veganism eventually go back to meat eating. So Hal Herzog, a psychology professor from Western Carolina University, decided to find out why. He ran a survey online and found that 35 percent stopped being vegetarian or vegan because they felt they were becoming less healthy; 25 percent cited the hassles or social stigma of being vegetarian; about 20 percent claimed they felt a strong urge to eat animal products; and 15 percent felt that not eating meat took a toll on their social life. In an article for *Psychology Today* online, Herzog described those participants who had "irresistible urges," saying that they

> talked about their protein cravings or how the smell of sizzling bacon would drive them crazy. One, for example, said "I just felt hungry all the time and that hunger would not be satisfied unless I ate meat." Another described his return to meat in mathematical terms: Starving college student + First night back home with the folks + Fifty or so blazin' buffalo wings waiting in the kitchen = Surrender.

Hal Herzog. "Why Do Most Vegetarians Go Back to Eating Meat?" *Animals and Us* (blog), *Psychology Today*, June 20, 2011. www.psychologytoday.com/blog/animals-and-us/201106/why-do-most-vegetarians-go-back-eating-meat.

Twenty percent of former vegans say they had irresistible urges to eat once-favorite animal products, such as these buffalo wings.

factories. I remember thinking when I was about 4 or 5 that it was funny that roast chickens were vaguely shaped like real, live chickens. I stopped eating red meat when I was about 19, because I found I had a problem with the fact that an animal that had feelings had to die for me to eat. Over the years, other foods [derived from animals] began to disgust me, and I stopped eating all meat and seafood.[23]

Other Shared Experiences

In whatever manner a person becomes a vegan, sooner or later he or she faces a second experience shared by all vegans—the necessity to decide whether or not to go beyond mere dietary practices and omit all animal products from their lives. Some feel that doing so is too limiting. Others say that some life-style habits are too hard to break. Many cannot imagine living

Many people who consider themselves vegans still eat dairy products because dairy products are made without killing the animal they come from.

without a certain item made from animal products; others might simply feel that there's no need to go as far as the ethical vegans do. Both Judy and Cheri fall into this category. Judy says, "I don't agree with strict veganism. [I] don't see any more harm in eating honey, which is produced by bees, than in eating fruit, which is produced by plants. I also eat eggs. [I] just make sure they are unfertilized. I drink a very small amount of milk in my tea. (I'm lactose intolerant.) As long as it doesn't hurt or kill an animal, I don't see a problem."[24]

Cheri cites different reasons for not cutting out all animal products, saying:

> I always state I have a vegan diet [as opposed to being a strict vegan]. I still wear the leather boots I bought for myself 15 years ago, or if I find a leather bag at the thrift shop [I buy it]. I do not buy new leather clothing/shoes if at all possible, but will accept gifts [made from animal parts]. All the foods that enter my body are vegan, including vitamins. I think it is more of a health choice, not a lifestyle.[25]

Other self-styled vegans eagerly plunge ahead and reject leather boots and bags, silk garments, specific cosmetics, and all other products made from animal parts. Gary L. Francione, for example, made that choice because he felt that "ethical veganism is the only sort of approach that results in consistent behavior." He maintains that "an ethical vegan sees veganism as a general approach to life—a philosophy of living—and not as merely a matter of lifestyle."[26]

Still another experience shared by all vegans is the ordeal of ordering a decent meal in a nonvegan restaurant. (The vast majority of restaurants are nonvegan.) Karen, the subject of an earlier interview, managed to get around this problem by simply ordering a salad and a side order of broccoli. It is not always that easy for vegans, however. Some restaurants either do not serve salads or, if they do, serve salads that are premade and contain cheese, bacon bits, or other animal products. Most restaurants do offer vegetable side dishes. But a vegan may not be in the mood for whatever vegetables happen to be on the menu. Or he or she may not like the way the vegetables are cooked.

According to several of the vegans interviewed in a recent survey, the lack of vegan offerings on most restaurant menus can be annoying. One of these respondents, Arlene, a housewife and mother of three in her forties, was asked whether it bothered her to sit down in a restaurant and find little or nothing on the menu for her to eat. "It doesn't so much bother me as disappoint me," she answered.

> It says something about the restaurant if they don't think about options for all their patrons, and it makes me feel they don't want my business. Another problem is that sometimes they will try to whip something up specially [for me], and it's usually pretty unimaginative and unflavorful—unseasoned broiled vegetables on a bed of bare pasta, as an example. Or they serve a vegetable burger, but on further questioning I find out it's cooked on the same cooking surface as their meat burgers. Usually, I will make a meal of sides—salad, a baked potato, and the vegetables of the day. Thumbs up to Burger King for their tasty veggie burger, microwaved separately![27]

Cool and Crazy Stuff

At home, in contrast, vegans are free to eat whatever foods and dishes they want, since their kitchens are stocked with the necessary vegan ingredients. Many nonvegans are surprised when they learn how long the list of these ingredients is. The common wisdom is that vegans are condemned to a highly restrictive diet with little variety and few tasty items. Yet the reality is quite different. Regarding the potential taste of vegan foods, "I consider my own pantry to be a food-lover's paradise," says Emmy-winning TV cook Christina Pirello. Her shelves are stacked with "vinegars, miso [a traditional Japanese seasoning] and exotic spices and natural condiments."[28]

Adopting Veganism Gradually

Many vegans say that they adopted their new diet and lifestyle gradually, sometimes over the course of several years. Matt, a longtime vegan advocate, suggests that becoming a vegan eater often works best when it occurs over the course of time, rather than all at once.

> The vegan lifestyle is an ongoing progression. Everyone should go at his or her own pace and remember that all steps towards veganism are positive. It is most important to focus on avoiding the products for which animals are bred and slaughtered. . . . When it comes to avoiding items that contain small amounts of [animal] byproducts, vegans must decide for themselves where to draw the line. Some vegans will adjust their level of abstinence according to the circumstances. For example, as a consumer, you might make sure the bread you buy is not made with whey; but as a dinner guest, you may accept bread without asking to see the ingredients. These types of compromises can actually hasten the spread of veganism, in that they help counter the attitude that it's very hard to be vegan.

> Quoted in Vegan Action. "Frequently Asked Questions." http://vegan.org/frequently-asked-questions.

Pirello goes on to explain that in addition to enjoying tasty foods, there is a wide range of staple foods a vegan can eat. "As you cook and fall in love with your new vegan life," she remarks, "you will naturally grow your list of staples and have all kinds of cool and crazy vegan stuff around to prepare great meals."[29] Among these staples are various grains and the breads and porridges made from them, including whole wheat bread, oatmeal, and other cereals. Vegans can also enjoy peanut butter and all-fruit jellies on their bread.

Among other common vegan staples and dishes are stir-fried vegetables, lentil soup, lentil stew, macaroni, spaghetti, most salad fixings, pancakes made without eggs, popcorn, vegetarian baked beans, fava beans, guacamole, tofu lasagna, spinach pies, and French toast made with soy milk. For people who are used to having burgers and hotdogs at cookouts, there are vegan equivalents, among them oat nut burgers, vegetable burgers, and soy hotdogs. In addition, for snacks and sometimes for dinner as well, vegans regularly eat pizza made without cheese and bean tacos made without cheese (which are also available at Taco Bell and other restaurants).

People with a sweet tooth can also enjoy vegan fare. In addition to apples, oranges, pears, plums, dates, figs, and other fruits, there are eggless cookies, soy ice cream, banana muffins, soy yogurt, rice pudding, frozen fruit desserts, corn fritters, pumpkin casserole, and the sweet Greek dessert baklava. A number of these desserts use nuts of various kinds, among the many wholesome foodstuffs that vegans eat to their heart's content. In the case of baklava and other desserts that normally employ honey, most vegans substitute a sticky syrup made from a mixture of natural sugar, concentrated fruit juices, and rose water.

The question of whether or not vegans should consume honey continues to be debated in the vegan community. Vegan Action, a group that promotes veganism to reduce animal suffering and improve human health, offers an overview of the issue and some commonsense advice. On whether or not honey is vegan, the group states:

> It depends on one's definition of vegan. Insects are animals, and so insect products, such as honey and silk, are not traditionally considered vegan. Many vegans, however, are not opposed to using insect products, because they do not believe insects are conscious of pain. . . . The question remains a matter of scientific debate and personal choice. However, when cooking

or labeling food for vegans—particularly vegans you don't know—it's best to be on the safe side and not include honey.[30]

"People Just like Us"

The food items cited above represent only some of the diverse staple foods that many vegans keep or prepare in their homes. These ingredients, along with a wide range of

Amount of Protein in Grains (Cooked)

Grain (1 cup)	Protein (Grams)
Amaranth	7
Barley, pearled	4 to 5
Barley, flakes	4
Buckwheat groats	5 to 6
Cornmeal (fine grind)	3
Cornmeal (polenta, coarse)	3
Millet, hulled	8.4
Oat Groats	6
Oat, bran	7
Quinoa	5
Rice, brown	3 to 5
Rice, white	4
Rice, wild	7
Rye, berries	7
Rye, flakes	6
Spelt, berries	5
Teff	6
Triticale	25
Wheat, whole berries	6 to 9
Couscous, whole wheat	6
Wheat, bulgur	5 to 6

Taken from: "Vegetarians in Paradise." www.vegparadise.com/protein.html.

The good taste and sheer variety of today's vegan foods and dishes, such as this tofu-based vegetables and noodles dish, makes converting to a vegan diet easier than one might think.

spices, can be combined to make thousands of appealing gourmet dishes. Some of the recipes in award-winning cookbook author Terry Hope Romero's popular volume *Vegan Eats World* include: Thai Shredded Mango Salad, French Farmhouse Asparagus Bisque, Greek Creamy Lemon Rice Soup, Coconut Black-Eyed Pea Curry, Lebanese Moussaka Stew, Coriander Rye Muffins, Roasted Tomatoes and Peppers Stuffed with Dill Rice, Lemon Garlic Potatoes, Sizzling Rice with Veggies and Chile Sauce, and Walnut Spice Sticky Cake.

According to Romero and other well-known vegans, the good taste and sheer variety of today's vegan foods and dishes make converting to a vegan diet easier than most people assume. "To the vegan curious," Romero says with a smile, "never mistake a rejection of eating animals as a rejection of really good-tasting food." Indeed, she states how proud she has become of her "vegan food community" in recent years. In her view, its members have shown a "willingness to push beyond what's expected of them and want something more. Evolving and in constant flux, vegan food is getting better, and we're better people for it. The more we open our plates to [meatless] food from around the world, the more likely we'll view others outside our culture as people just like us!"[31]

CHAPTER 3

Vegan Nutrition and Health

Proper nutrition and health are fundamental aspects of all well-rounded diets, vegan and nonvegan alike. In the last few decades, therefore, as the number of vegans around the globe has significantly increased, the health benefits as well as potential risks of vegan eating have been studied. The results of these studies have been analyzed and discussed by trained dietitians, including those belonging to the Vegetarian Nutrition Dietetic Practice Group, a wing of the Academy of Nutrition and Dietetics (formerly the American Dietetic Association).

So far, adopting a vegan diet has been found to be nutritionally beneficial and safe, as long as the person who adopts the diet is careful to consume the right foods in the right amounts. Yet this has sometimes proved problematic. Even some of the staunchest vegans admit that some of their fellow vegans fail at this endeavor. It is "quite possible to develop a variety of nutrient deficiencies on a vegan diet," Erik Marcus, author of *The Ultimate Vegan Guide*, writes. "What's worse, some of these deficiencies can creep up on you. They may take years to manifest, and by the time you realize something's wrong, irreversible damage may have occurred."[32]

Complicating matters is the fact that in some circles, veganism still retains a reputation as odd and/or extreme.

Disagreements are ongoing between strict vegans and the more vocal defenders of traditional meat eating. The latter are not fully convinced that a strict vegan diet can be nutritionally sound.

The Challenge of Getting Enough Nutrients

Supporting the vegan side of this dispute, the Academy of Nutrition and Dietetics and other respected scientific and medical organizations insist that a carefully planned vegan diet can be healthy. This has helped to fuel a flurry of books on vegan nutrition and cooking in recent years. Their authors frequently and vigorously promote adopting a vegan diet and lifestyle.

In fact, some leading vegans suggest it is not *vegan* eating that should be doubted and criticized, but rather the traditional nonvegan diet built around meat and other animal products. The standard American diet, they argue, is potentially less healthy than a well-designed vegan diet. Among the louder critics of meat eating has been Marcus himself, who suggests that consistently consuming animal flesh can be a "slippery slope" to poor health. He continues:

> Nearly all healthy people can likely tolerate a couple roasted pieces of chicken a week without suffering adverse health consequences. The trouble is that it's easy to go from eating a little chicken to making things like ice cream, pepperoni pizza, and burgers a regular part of your diet. Sadly, no alarm bell starts ringing when a person passes his or her individual risk threshold. Instead, the damage silently accumulates, year by year, in the forms of gradually clogging arteries and significantly increased cancer and diabetes risk. The beauty of a vegan diet is that it slams the door shut on all animal products, so you never have to wonder if your personal risk threshold has been exceeded.[33]

Marcus goes on to make a detailed and strongly worded case that vegan nutrition is healthier for people than the nutrition derived from the traditional American diet, which

Gourmet Living Cuisine **matt amsden**

Many vegan cookbooks have been published that include recipes containing all the nutrients that a human needs.

is built around animal products. "Compared to a typical omnivorous diet," he says, "a vegan diet is generally lower in fat. Vegans also usually eat more health-promoting fruits and veggies than omnivores, and they don't have to worry about the scary carcinogens that may form when meat is cooked."[34]

Many critics of veganism are quick to provide a counter-argument. They readily agree that a diet high in fatty animal products and low in vegetables and fruits is often unhealthy. They also concur that the foods in a typical vegan diet are fundamentally nutritious. The problem, these critics say, is that some vegans may not get enough, or the right balance, of the nutrients necessary for good health. An article in the online culinary magazine *StarChefs.com* points out that "although vegan diets are undoubtedly beneficial in certain respects, they are detrimental in others, causing minor to serious health problems that often go unnoticed." The article adds that "even the most informed, health-conscious vegans run the risk of malnutrition. There are several nutrients that are found in abundance in animal products, but exist in only a handful of vegan foods. Therefore, critics argue, while it is possible to get all of the essential nutrients on a vegan diet, it is extremely challenging."[35]

Is Veganism Natural?

Those who contend that it is hard to obtain all the necessary nutrients on a vegan diet sometimes go further and suggest that veganism is not natural. That is, human beings evolved to eat both meat and plants, which made them omnivores. Christopher Wanjek, a science spokesperson for NBC News, points to a recent study of the brain sizes of primates, which was published in the prestigious journal *Proceedings of the National Academy of Sciences*. Its findings, he says, suggest that meat eating enabled the brains of human ancestors to grow significantly over a period of only a few million years. This and other related studies, he writes, show

> that it would have been biologically implausible for humans to evolve such a large brain on a raw, vegan diet and that meat-eating was a crucial element of

Sources of Guidelines on Vegan Nutrition

The expanding research into vegan diets and nutrition in the past few decades has provided vital health and nutritional guidelines for people converting from the standard omnivorous diet to a vegan one. Some of the most informative books about vegan nutrition have been published by Winston Craig, Debra Wasserman, and Reed Mangels. Also, noted dietitian Suzanne Havala has worked with the Academy of Nutrition and Dietetics to establish basic, reliable facts about vegan nutrition. A subgroup of that organization, the Vegetarian Nutrition Dietetic Practice Group, was established in 1991. Its members, based in the United States, Canada, and several other countries, provide reliable information and the latest studies about vegan nutrition. According to the American Vegan Society, among the leading researchers into vegan diets have been Michael Klaper, author of *Vegan Nutrition: Pure and Simple*, and William Harris, who wrote *The Scientific Basis of Vegetarianism*. Also, important studies about vegan health and nutrition were carried out by members of the Seventh-Day Adventist Church both in England and North America.

human evolution at least 1 million years before the dawn of humankind. At the core of this research is the understanding that the modern human brain consumes 20 percent of the body's energy at rest, twice that of other primates. Meat and cooked foods were needed to provide the necessary calorie boost to feed a growing brain.[36]

Not surprisingly, several vegans refuse to accept this assertion that the human species is omnivorous by nature. Brian Patton, author of a well-known vegan cookbook, asks:

> Are we meant to consume animal products? Is it optimal for our longevity? I think not. Humans are thought to be omnivores, just like the grizzly [bear]. . . . I'll tell you what. You show me the guy who can chase down a deer on foot, kill it with his bare hands, tear through its flesh with his own teeth, and digest the raw innards every day without getting ill . . . and I'll reconsider my stance. Based on the logic of the animal kingdom, we are designed to eat plants. Our teeth are dull, our jaws are weak, and eating raw animal flesh usually makes us sick. The tools we are born with lend themselves to obtaining and digesting food that doesn't increase cholesterol, have unnecessary fats, or try to run away or bite us back.[37]

Joanne Stepaniak agrees. She reasons that humans are not naturally carnivorous in part because they have a longer digestive system than meat-eating animals. The longer system allows people to extract more nutrients from foods than does the carnivores' shorter system, which is designed to let meat pass through the body before turning rancid. Also, she argues, "the low levels of acidity in our stomachs are in stark contrast to the high levels in meat-eaters. Although we have incisors capable of tearing flesh, I have

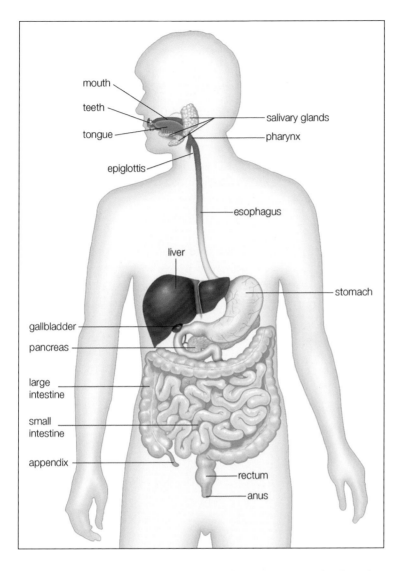

mouth
teeth
tongue
epiglottis
salivary glands
pharynx
esophagus
liver
stomach
gallbladder
pancreas
large intestine
small intestine
appendix
rectum
anus

Humans have a longer digestive system than do strictly meat-eating animals, which, some say, shows that humans were meant to be vegetarians.

always thought that these were for cropping the harder vegetables. [In addition] we do not have claws or talons for tearing flesh."[38]

The Question of Nutritional Shortfalls

While this debate over whether humans are naturally omnivorous or herbivorous goes on, medical researchers and doctors representing both sides have turned their attention to specific nutrients that all people need to be healthy. Leading vegan writers admit they must be careful to consume

Worries About Malnutrition

Some medical authorities worry that some societal groups may be more likely than others to suffer from malnutrition and that adopting a strict vegan diet may not be healthy for members of these groups. Drew Ramsey, a professor of psychiatry at Columbia University, sums up this argument:

> Certain populations that are particularly susceptible to inadequate nutrition should think twice about veganism, including adolescents, the elderly, the poor, pregnant women, and those with psychiatric or chronic medical illnesses. . . . While it is common among vegans to take synthetic supplements to make up for the lack of animal nutrients in their diets, studies suggest that supplements are ineffective substitutes for real food and carry significant health risks of their own. Supplements are also expensive, and people tend to take them irregularly, so while a strict vegan diet with supplements may be possible with proper medical supervision, for most people it's neither practical nor desirable.

Drew Ramsey. "Meat Is Brain Food." *New York Times,* August 17, 2012. www.nytimes.com/roomforde bate/2012/04/17/is-veganism-good-for-everyone/meat -is-brain-food.

Many vegans take dietary supplements to ensure that they are receiving complete nutrition.

enough of the nutrients that are scarce in plant foods. These nutrients, including iron, zinc, calcium, omega-3 (also called n-3) fatty acids, and vitamins B_{12} and D, constitute the classic shortfalls of a vegan diet.

The central question regarding these substances is whether it is possible to consume enough of them consistently for an entire lifetime to ensure proper nutrition and good health. The Academy of Nutrition and Dietetics addressed this question to some degree in 2009, saying:

> Appropriately planned vegetarian diets, including total vegetarian or vegan diets, are healthful, nutritionally adequate, and may provide health benefits in the prevention and treatment of certain diseases. Well-planned vegetarian diets are appropriate for individuals during all stages of the life cycle, including . . . infancy, childhood, and adolescence, and for athletes. A vegetarian diet is defined as one that does not include meat (including fowl) or seafood, or products containing those foods. [In regard] to key nutrients for vegetarians including protein, n-3 fatty acids, iron, zinc, iodine, calcium, and vitamins D and B-12, a vegetarian diet can meet current recommendations for all of these nutrients. In some cases, supplements or fortified foods can provide useful amounts of important nutrients.[39]

Thus, the academy says, it is possible for a person to adopt a vegan diet and get enough of the substances that make up the classic vegan nutritional shortfalls. Yet some medical professionals emphasize that, although this is possible, it is not necessarily easy. A person must be constantly vigilant day after day, month after month, and year after year to ensure he or she is getting enough of these nutrients. The very fact that the academy mentioned the possible need to take fortified foods or supplements, critics say, should be seen as a red flag. One such critic is Drew Ramsey, a professor of psychiatry at Columbia University. Worried that a vegan diet can adversely affect the human brain, he warns, "Clinical research finds that people on vegan diets commonly suffer from a variety of nutritional deficiencies. One study, for instance, showed that more than half of vegans tested were deficient in vitamin B_{12}, putting them at risk of mental health problems such as fatigue, poor concentration, decreased brain volume with aging, and irreversible nerve damage." It would be better, Ramsey states,

> to modify the vegan diet with a minimal amount of animal nutrients from responsibly raised, high-quality sources, perhaps local seafood or grass-fed lamb. Those with ethical objections to killing animals can meet all their animal-nutrient needs with dairy products from grass-fed cows [that are allowed to die of natural causes], organic eggs from cage-free chickens, and occasional servings of mussels or oysters.[40]

Dealing with the Shortfalls

Large numbers of vegans disagree with Ramsey that it is either necessary or prudent to supplement their plant-based diets with a few selected animal-based foods. These individuals feel that a serious and responsible person who decides to adopt a vegan diet will have the ability to make sure he or she is getting proper nutrition. When asked how she deals with the classic vegan dietary shortfalls, for instance, Judy shrugged and said, "I've never had this come up. My blood tests have always come back normal. I personally believe that milk products are bad for humans, and have avoided them for years because of being lactose intolerant, yet I have minimal bone loss."[41]

When asked the same question, Cheri was less complacent but equally sure that she had this potential problem under control. "In order to ensure all of my body's needs are covered," she responded, "I am cognizant of the vitamins and minerals needed in my daily intake. To be sure, I included iron rich foods like raisins and spinach, as well as a vegan supplement. For calcium, broccoli is a staple in my diet as well, along with a supplement. Zinc and the B vitamins are gained with vitamins on a daily basis."[42]

HEALTH FACT

The Vegetarian Resource Group says that good sources of plant-based protein include oatmeal, soy milk, whole wheat bread, peanut butter, tofu, almonds, broccoli, and brown rice.

Good Sources of Calcium

Source	Serving Size	
Soy or rice milk, commercial, calcium-fortified, plain	8 oz	200–300 mg
Collard greens, cooked	1 cup	357 mg
Blackstrap molasses	2 tbsp	400 mg
Tofu, processed with calcium sulfate	4 oz	200–330 mg
Calcium-fortified orange juice	8 oz	300 mg
Tofu, processed with nigari	4 oz	80–230 mg
Kale, cooked	1 cup	179 mg
Tahini	2 tbsp	128 mg
Almonds	1/4 cup	89 mg

Taken from: Vegetarian Resource Group. "Veganism in a Nutshell." www.vrg.org/nutshell/vegan.htm#books.

In contrast, Alan said he did not trust taking supplements, even those advertised and labeled "vegan." He prefers to go the "all natural way," in his words, and get all of his nutrients from plant-based foods. "My calcium comes mostly from orange juice, tofu, and green vegetables, which I eat a lot of,"[43] he reported.

Like several other national or international vegan organizations, the Vegetarian Resource Group (VRG) offers abundant information about which plant-based foods are rich in

Orange juice and tofu are good sources of nondairy calcium.

calcium and the other nutrients on the vegan shortfall list. To get enough zinc, the VRG's website states, one should make sure to eat plenty of nuts, grains, and legumes (fruit-like foods that grow from pods, including lentils, peas, clover, beans, and alfalfa). Meanwhile, the VRG explains, iron is fairly abundant in a wide range of natural, plant-based foods. Among these are dark-green leafy vegetables, raisins, dried beans, lentils, soybeans, prune juice, kidney beans, peas, millet, kale, and watermelon.

Another nutrient on the shortfall list, vitamin B_{12}, is a bit more difficult to obtain in sufficient amounts, the VRG says. One approach is to buy a product called Red Star nutritional yeast, also called Vegetarian Support Formula, and follow the directions on the label. Vegans can also get their vitamin B_{12} from fortified soy milk and supplemental tablets. Dietary or partial vegans who consume small amounts of animal products can get their vitamin B_{12} from eggs and various dairy products. Foodstuffs such as tofu, soybeans, walnuts, canola oil, flaxseed, and flaxseed oil are sources of omega-3 fatty acids, another controversial nutrient sometimes lacking in a vegan diet.

Finally, just like nonvegans, vegans must make sure they absorb enough vitamin D to maintain good health. For partial vegans, vitamin D is easily obtainable from milk and other dairy products. But strict vegans refuse to consume dairy products, so they must get their vitamin D from other sources. One approach is to buy soy or rice milk that has been fortified with vitamin D. Another route preferred by ethical vegans is the most natural one—namely, to expose oneself to sunlight. When sunlight falls on the skin, the body produces vitamin D, and all that is needed for good health is to let the face and hands absorb sunlight for fifteen minutes or so two or three times a week.

Feeling Better

The VRG and other vegan groups that provide such nutritional information assume, or at least hope, that vegans who read it will be responsible and consistent enough to ensure they are eating the right amounts of the right foods. Critics point out that there is no way to guarantee this, however. It

To get enough zinc, one should make sure to eat plenty of nuts, grains, and legumes (e.g., peas, beans, and alfalfa).

is a matter of medical record that doctors and hospitals deal with an undetermined number of cases of malnutrition each year caused by strict vegan diets.

Yet on the flip side of this nutritional coin is the fact that large numbers of vegans *are* getting proper nutrition. This seems to be verified by their affirmations that they felt noticeably better, both physically and mentally, after converting to veganism. "The changes in my body since switching to a vegan diet are quite noticeable," Cheri reports.

> I do feel better, physically and emotionally. I have had staff from the doctor's office comment on my "textbook" numbers for cholesterol count, as well as blood pressure. I feel lighter after eating, as well as more satisfied. I know all the ingredients when making a meal, and am aware of the health benefits of everything I choose to eat. . . . Since becoming vegan, my skin is clearer, I seldom experience any indigestion, and overall have been sick very rarely.[44]

Other vegans claim they experienced even more dramatic health benefits after switching to veganism. A woman named Julie says, "I had no idea the health benefits that would follow! My goodness. [My] migraines: gone! What I thought were allergy symptoms: gone!"[45] Another vegan, David, states, "I used to get sick a lot. Since becoming vegan I don't. . . . Going vegan is like a breath of fresh air and life just makes sense!"[46] Still another contented vegan, Billy, says that ever since becoming a vegan he has had no indigestion, gas, constipation, skin problems, aching joints, or bad breath. "I am a new man!"[47] he boasts.

Only a handful of vegans make these claims, of course. There is no way to know whether all vegans have enjoyed such improvements in their health. For the moment, these highly satisfied vegans might be thought of as balancing out the ones who were diagnosed as malnourished by their doctors. Another way to think about it is to acknowledge that adopting a vegan diet remains a controversial choice and that those who do choose it must take responsibility for making sure they get proper nutrition.

CHAPTER 4

Ideas Behind Ethical Veganism

Strict, or ethical, vegans say that they adopted and maintain their vegan diet not simply for the benefits of good health, but also—indeed primarily—for moral reasons. They ethically oppose the exploitation and killing of nonhuman creatures by humans for the purpose of eating those creatures. Vegans' strongly held beliefs in this regard are rooted in a concept called speciesism, basically defined as an arrogant disregard for the well-being of other sentient species.

The term *sentient* is used in different ways by different people. But in this context, it describes beings who can to one degree or another think, feel pain and loss, and feel and exhibit love and loyalty not only to members of their own species, but also in many cases to humans. Vegans hold that virtually all mammals fall into this category, and they usually include most nonmammals as well.

Thus, ethical vegans adhere to a philosophy that condemns all forms of animal exploitation and cruelty and view themselves as "antispeciesists." The well-known Pulitzer Prize–winning journalist Chris Hedges, who is an ethical vegan, eloquently sums up this activist philosophy:

> We need to stop deceiving ourselves that nonhumans are "things"; that because they are not "like us" they do not matter. We need to stop denying their sentience

and deceiving ourselves their sentience does not matter. We need to stop deceiving ourselves that nonhumans only have an interest in serving us; that they are our "happy slaves"; that they have no interest in continuing life, only an interest in not suffering and that murdering them is acceptable. That's a lie and we know it. Nonhuman animals have an interest in relationships, they protect and care for their young, they have their own purpose, they suffer, they love life and do not want to die, and they have an interest in living free of exploitation. As individuals, we need to stop perpetuating this lie, this speciesist indoctrination that exploiting the vulnerable and the innocent is acceptable and justifiable.[48]

Vegans believe that mammals are sentient and that in general no animals should be treated cruelly by humans.

Doing Their Best

Nonvegan critics of this ethical vegan philosophy say it is too extreme, as well as unrealistic. Thousands of animals die every day in the course of growing and harvesting crops that vegans eat, the critics say. Insects and other small animals hiding in tall grass are caught in harvesting machines or crushed under tractor wheels, while others die when new croplands destroy their habitats. According to the critics, therefore, vegans save some animals while allowing others to die terrible deaths.

One vegan counterargument to this critique is that the animals that die in agricultural pursuits are not killed purposefully, nor are they eaten, nor were they raised specifically to be slaughtered and eaten. Some ethical vegans admit that they cannot save every animal. But by eating a plant-based diet, they can at least save some.

The admission by some vegans that humans cannot save all animals from unnecessary deaths underscores the fact that the ethical vegan philosophy rests on idealistic principles. That is, a strict vegan knows that his or her choice to give up eating meat can save only a limited number of sentient creatures. Ethical vegans are doing their best, they say, to uphold their beliefs, and they hope that other animals will be saved when other nonvegans convert to veganism. Therefore, adopting a vegan diet and lifestyle is as much symbolic as it is realistic.

Some nonvegans are untroubled by human exploitation of animals, seeing it as part of nature's plan. For this reason, and also because they assume the efforts of vegans save only a small percentage of animals from abuse, these critics view veganism as unrealistic and useless. In contrast, others—vegans and nonvegans alike—see it as principled and brave, a clear example of having the courage to stand up for one's convictions. Yet arguments about whether ethical veganism is realistic or unrealistic, useless or courageous, are irrelevant

HEALTH FACT

One of the biggest problems with the way animals are treated in the factory farm system, vegan activist Erik Marcus, says, is that meat, milk, and eggs taste roughly the same when the creatures are well-treated as when they are poorly treated. Treating them well costs more money, he suggests, which the factory owners are usually reluctant to spend.

to the goal of comprehending the ethical vegans' perspective. To understand why people become vegan, one must more closely examine the ideas they embrace and the practices they condemn.

Some Horrifying Scenarios

Few modern public figures have explained why they embraced veganism more clearly and more powerfully than well-known vegan advocate and animal rights activist Dan Cudahy. He became a vegan, he stated in an often-cited passage from one of his essays,

> because after much learning and thought about the issue, I have come to see enslaving, exploiting, or intentionally killing an animal as morally equivalent to enslaving, exploiting, or intentionally killing a child. The only difference is one is socially acceptable and the other is socially unacceptable. That may sound shocking or "extreme" to some people, but it is only because we are acculturated [raised with certain ideas and values] to devalue sentient nonhuman beings to the status of

"things." What is truly extreme is the violence of intentionally killing 10 billion land animals annually in the U.S. (56 billion annually globally) for unnecessary food preferences alone. Unless you consider nonviolence and justice to be "extreme," veganism is not extreme.[49]

Cudahy and many other ethical vegans view this killing of animals for food as repugnant and morally wrong. Moreover, it is not merely the killing of the creatures that they object to. The words *cruelty* and *animal suffering* are regularly leveled by vegans at the modern factory farm system, which produces most of the meat people consume. Vegan activists claim that a majority of the cows, pigs, and chickens people eat suffer through a great deal of brutal, inhumane treatment *before* they are slaughtered.

First, according to Cudahy and other vegan activists, most such animals are confined in cages or pens where they are crowded together so closely that their bodies are nearly touching. This crowding is especially pronounced for millions of

Seeking a Moral Life

The ethical aspects of refraining from eating meat were addressed by the great Russian writer Leo Tolstoy. "Seeking for self-control," he wrote,

a man will inevitably follow one definite sequence, and in this sequence the first thing will be self-control in food—fasting. And in fasting, if he be really and seriously seeking to live a good life, the first thing from which he will abstain will always be the use of animal food, because, to say nothing of the excitation of the passions caused by such food, its use is simply immoral, as it involves the performance of an act which is contrary to the moral feeling—killing; and is called forth only by greediness and the desire for tasty food. The precise reason why abstinence from animal food will be the first act of fasting and of a moral life is admirably explained . . . not by one man only, but by all mankind in the persons of its best representatives during all the conscious life of humanity.

Leo Tolstoy. "The First Step." International Vegetarian Union. www.ivu.org/history/tolstoy/the_%20first_step.html.

chickens raised in so-called battery cages. Typically, each bird spends most of its life standing or sitting in a space smaller than a single sheet of notebook paper. This makes it impossible for the chicken to fully stretch its wings or to enjoy other natural behaviors.

Another common practice documented within the battery cage system by animal welfare activists is the burning off of young chicks' beaks without benefit of painkillers. Meanwhile, workers regularly seize chickens by their throats and throw them into the cages. Still other recorded abuses include allowing the birds to suffer from open wounds without treatment; failing to remove dead chickens from cages and leaving their bodies to rot alongside living birds; and suffocating unwanted live chicks in plastic bags or grinding them up in machines without any regard for their terror and suffering.

The raising of pigs in the factory farm system has also been singled out as cruel by animal rights activists. Vegan Outreach reports several horrifying scenarios, including the following one:

> Piglets in confinement operations are weaned from their mothers [only 2 to 3 weeks] after birth, compared with 13 weeks [under normal conditions], because they gain weight faster on their hormone- and antibiotic-fortified feed. This premature weaning leaves the pigs with a lifelong craving to suck and chew, a desire they gratify in confinement by biting the tail of the animal in front of them. A normal pig would fight off his molester, but a demoralized pig has stopped caring. . . . Tens of thousands of hogs spend their entire lives ignorant of sunshine or earth or straw, crowded together beneath a metal roof upon metal slats suspended over a manure pit. So it's not surprising that an animal as sensitive and intelligent as a pig would get depressed, and a depressed pig will allow his tail to be chewed on to the point of infection. Sick pigs [like these] are clubbed to death on the spot.[50]

Efforts to Stop Animal Cruelty

Various vegan and nonvegan organizations, as well as numerous veterinarians across the Western world, continually object to such practices and call on leaders within the food industry to stop them. Typical is a statement of protest by Lee Schrader, a veterinarian in Dayton, Ohio, who has performed many postmortem exams on animal victims of abuse and neglect. "The unnecessary violence," she says, along with the "unskilled killing, and especially the extreme confinement and deprivation of the most minimal and basic needs of the hens cannot be allowed to continue. Battery cage confinement of laying hens is nothing short of torture."[51]

That the complaints and campaigns of activists have helped to alleviate at least some of this cruelty is supported

Millions of chickens are raised in so-called battery cages like these. Typically, each bird spends most of its life standing or sitting in a space smaller than a single sheet of notebook paper. For some people, veganism is a protest of such treatment.

by some recent events in the food industry. The California-based organization Mercy for Animals reports:

> Battery cages are so cruel that the entire European Union and the [U.S.] states of California and Michigan have banned their use. Additionally, leading food retailers, such as Whole Foods, Hellmann's, Wolfgang Puck, and Subway, and hundreds of colleges and universities refuse to use or sell eggs from hens subjected to the inherent abuses of battery cages.[52]

Although vegans and other animal welfare activists welcome these positive moves, they caution that they have barely made a dent in the cruel practices of the enormous factory farm industry. In part this is because decisions to refrain from these methods are mostly voluntarily for factories and companies. "Sadly," a spokesperson for Mercy for Animals remarks, "not a single federal law currently provides any protection to birds at the hatchery, on the factory farm, or during slaughter. Further, most states [have] sweeping exemptions for farmed animals, which allow for abuses to run rampant without prosecution."[53]

The Case for Promoting Veganism

The absence of laws against animal cruelty in the factory farm industry frustrates many people, and some of these concerned individuals have turned to veganism. Faced with such frustration and concern, "it can be far easier," Erik Marcus says, "to simply transition to a vegan diet. There's a great deal of satisfaction that comes with sitting down to a delicious meal and knowing that not a single animal has suffered to produce it."[54]

The Vegan Society concurs that disgust with the current manner in which animal products are produced is the core reason that most vegans chose their diet and lifestyle. "Millions of calves and male chicks [are] killed every year as 'waste products' of milk and egg production," the society states on its website. "Choosing a vegan diet is a daily demonstration of compassion for all these creatures."[55]

Some ethical vegans feel that this demonstration of compassion should be directed as often as possible at nonvegans. That is, passionate vegans should actively promote their vegan beliefs in hopes of expanding the vegan community and thereby further reducing the incidence of animal cruelty. Cudahy is a major advocate of this approach. "As vegan advocates," he says,

veganism is the message we should exclusively and unequivocally promote. Anything less . . . betrays the

A vegan lies covered in barbecue sauce as part of a demonstration to raise public awareness about the mistreatment of animals used for food.

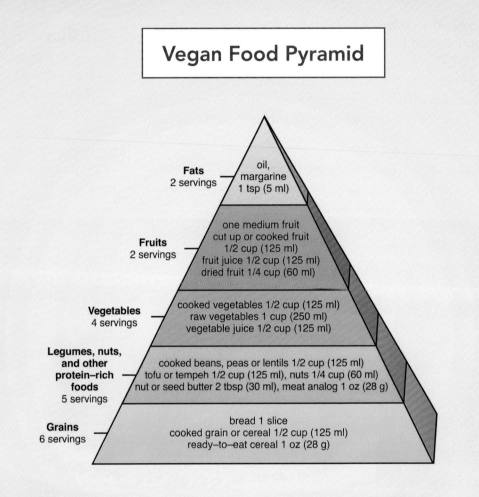

Vegan Food Pyramid

Fats
2 servings — oil, margarine 1 tsp (5 ml)

Fruits
2 servings — one medium fruit cut up or cooked fruit 1/2 cup (125 ml) fruit juice 1/2 cup (125 ml) dried fruit 1/4 cup (60 ml)

Vegetables
4 servings — cooked vegetables 1/2 cup (125 ml) raw vegetables 1 cup (250 ml) vegetable juice 1/2 cup (125 ml)

Legumes, nuts, and other protein–rich foods
5 servings — cooked beans, peas or lentils 1/2 cup (125 ml) tofu or tempeh 1/2 cup (125 ml), nuts 1/4 cup (60 ml) nut or seed butter 2 tbsp (30 ml), meat analog 1 oz (28 g)

Grains
6 servings — bread 1 slice cooked grain or cereal 1/2 cup (125 ml) ready–to–eat cereal 1 oz (28 g)

Taken from: www.zazzle.com/diagram_of_a_vegan_diet_food_pyramid_poster-228089866688914750.

fundamental truth that brings us to veganism in the first place—the understanding that we must bring an end to all [animal] exploitation if we are to move beyond the pandemic of violence that underlies our current cultural paradigm [model or pattern].[56]

As is the case with any set of beliefs promoted by an individual or group, prospective converts want to know what is being advocated. Usually, they seek to discover exactly what veganism is all about, including the principles that serious vegans live by. For this reason, several vegan activists have compiled lists of principles or rules to live by. One of the better-known versions in the American vegan community is that posted by ethical vegan and animal rights activist Trisha Roberts on the *Veganism Is Nonviolence* blog. Her rules are an attempt to define what she and her fellow activists call an abolitionist approach to animal rights. Briefly stated, these principles are:

> All sentient beings, humans or nonhumans, have one right: the basic right not to be treated as the property of others. Our recognition of the one basic right means that we must abolish, and not merely regulate, institutionalized animal exploitation—because it assumes that animals are the property of humans. Just as we reject racism, sexism, ageism, and heterosexism, we reject speciesism.... We reject any campaign that promotes sexism, racism, heterosexism, or other forms of discrimination against humans. We recognize that the most important step that any of us can take toward abolition is to adopt the vegan lifestyle and to educate others about veganism.... We recognize the principle of nonviolence as the guiding principle of the animal rights movement. Violence is the problem; it is not any part of the solution.[57]

Converting by Example

Wide differences of opinion on various issues exist among the millions of vegans in the world, and no two vegans think exactly alike. So it should not be a surprise to find that some vegans disagree with the notion that they have a duty to convert other people to their beliefs. When asked whether she thought it was right or wrong to do so, Arlene answered, "It's wrong. I would prefer to convert by example. I think everyone has a right to his/her own opinion, and deserves the right to be free from others' preaching. It's just as wrong for me to try to convert others as it is for the people who wave steaks in front of my face. Everyone needs to follow his or her own path. Neither my husband nor daughter has chosen veganism."[58]

Cheri answered the same question similarly. "I am the only vegan in my family," she said.

> I still prepare meat for my husband and children. I believe it is not my place to convert anyone. I prepare my vegan meals and share [them] with my family. Some of the [vegan] meals they really enjoy and prefer over meat meals. My decision to become and remain with a vegan diet is mine, and the respect is returned. My family does not try to coerce me into returning to animal foods. If anyone is interested, I share my dishes and desserts. If they like it, great, [but] if not, that's okay too. It's all about having an open mind and seeing there is more than the old standby of meat and potatoes for dinner.[59]

A Call for More Education

Some vegans who hold the opposite view and advocate active promotion of veganism hope to see major improvements in the treatment of animals in the food industry during their lifetimes. Others, however, are more conservative in their predictions. They acknowledge that even if they promoted their beliefs day and night and each year more and more people accepted them, ending animal cruelty and meat eating would not be a quick and easy process.

Indeed, Cudahy himself, one of the more vocal advocates of veganism, tries to be realistic. In his writings he recognizes that humans were mostly meat eaters for hundreds or perhaps even thousands of generations. So the desire, along with the very idea, of consuming meat and other animal products is deeply ingrained in society and perhaps within the human psyche, too. The existence of millions of vegans and their efforts to help animals are fairly recent phenomena, he says. As a result, it may take a very long time to erase society's views on speciesism

Are Animals Actually Saved?

Some nonvegans feel that the ethical vegans' attempt to avoid the killing of animals by consuming only plant-based foods is unrealistic. This view is summarized by journalist Ward Clark, who claims that large numbers of animals are killed in the production of crops that vegans readily eat.

Unfortunately for the ethical vegan, the production of food alone reduces the claim to impossibility. Animals are killed in untold millions in the course of plant agriculture. Some are killed accidentally in the course of mechanized farming; some killed deliberately in the course of pest control. Animals are killed every day. Every potato, every stick of celery, every cup of rice, and every carrot has a blood trail leading from field to plate. . . . Pheasants and rabbits are routinely killed in planting and harvesting, and rodents are killed by the thousands using traps and pesticides at every step: production, storage, and transportation. Rational people know this and don't worry about it. It's an inevitable consequence of modern, high-production agriculture. The ethical vegan, when confronted with these undeniable facts, collapses. Their reaction, in almost every case, is to do a rhetorical lateral arabesque into a new claim, that their vegan diet somehow causes "less death and suffering" than a non-vegan diet, a ridiculous and unsupportable argument.

Ward Clark. "The Myth of the 'Ethical Vegan.'" *PJMedia* (blog), October 23, 2011. http://pjmedia.com/blog/the-myth-of-the-ethical-vegan.

Many believe that meat animals like these calves will not be quickly saved by someone's adopting of a vegan lifestyle.

and meat eating. "It will take a gradual understanding," Cudahy states,

> and a wearing down of the cultural prejudice of speciesism via relentless educational efforts over many years on the part of many vegan advocates. That is why the quest for new vegans who reject speciesism is so important. We need more vegan educators. The prejudice of speciesism will have to become as familiar in society as the prejudice of racism. I think it is impossible to know how long it will take. Social change can be amazingly rapid and exponential, but it can also remain stagnant or go the other way. Like the weather, it is unpredictable. For now, it largely depends on how quickly vegetarians go vegan and vegans embrace abolitionism and vegan education.[60]

CHAPTER 5

Vegans and the Environment

Large numbers of vegans worry about the environment, and some of them speak out about the many issues related to keeping the environment clean and safe for both humans and animals. Strict vegans maintain that many of the ways that humans raise animals for meat negatively affect the environment. They regularly call attention to such problems as water waste and pollution, soil pollution and depletion, climate change (global warming), and the creation of dangerous new bacteria that can sicken or kill unsuspecting people.

The contention of vegans who keep track of such problems is that large-scale meat eating makes those problems worse and thereby hurts the planet on a regular basis. The widely respected Worldwatch Institute, an independent research group devoted to global environmental concerns, agrees, stating, "The human appetite for animal flesh is a driving force behind virtually every major category of environmental damage now threatening the human future—deforestation, erosion, fresh water scarcity, air and water pollution, climate change, biodiversity loss, [and] the spread of disease."[61]

It should be noted that the institute is careful to say that meat eating is "a" driving force behind such dire problems.

Reputable scientists concur that there are several other causes for these environmental problems besides raising animals for their meat. Among others, they include emissions of greenhouse gases from cars, trucks, and factories, illegal dumping of hazardous wastes, and the rapid destruction of forests to meet the needs of growing human populations.

Still, a quick look at only one of these issues—climate change—shows that meeting the demands of billions of human meat eaters does cause a significant portion of the problem. In 2006 the Agriculture and Consumer Protection Department of the United Nations (UN) announced the results of studies conducted on worldwide animal agriculture. According to the studies, raising cattle, pigs, and other large creatures produces 18 percent, or nearly a fifth, of the total amount of greenhouse gases emitted into the atmosphere. That includes 37 percent of the methane and 65 percent of the nitrogen oxides that enter the air each year—impressive figures. (These and other greenhouse gases, especially carbon dioxide, help trap warmth in the atmosphere, similar to the way glass traps warmth in a greenhouse.)

Worldwatch Institute president Lester Brown asserts that human's appetites for meat is at the root of environmental damage—from deforestation to air and water pollution to the spread of disease.

Vegans believe not only that meat eating makes such problems worse, but also, in a more positive light, that adopting a vegan diet helps alleviate them. "From an environmental perspective, a switch to a vegan diet makes a lot of sense," Erik Marcus says on his popular vegan website. "This is especially true where beef and fish are concerned."[62]

Water and Land Waste

Leading vegan organization Vegan Action briefly sums up the case that meat eating is ultimately bad for both the environment and society. First, it says, precious resources that could otherwise be used to feed starving people in poor countries are wasted on raising animals for their meat: "Animal agriculture takes a devastating toll on the earth. It is an inefficient way of producing food, since feed for farm animals requires water, land, fertilizer, and other resources that could otherwise have been used directly for producing human food."[63]

Taking the issue of water use first, scientists and farmers agree that raising farm animals requires large amounts of water. These creatures include those that are slaughtered for their meat. The question is whether most of the residents of the United States and other nations in which meat eating is common agree that raising farm animals is enough of a benefit to justify the use of this much water. Since the majority of people in the world continue to eat meat, it appears that they do. The same case might be made for land use. Raising animals requires large amounts of land and good soil for grazing and growing feed grains; many countries appear content to allocate huge tracts of land to these uses.

Vegans are decidedly *not* content to use water and land in these ways. They want to see what they view as thoughtless and wasteful environmental practices steadily phased out. Another leading vegan group, Vegan Outreach, makes this case:

> The typical North American diet, with its large share of animal products, requires twice as much water to produce as the less meat-intensive diets common in

many Asian and some European countries. Eating lower on the food chain could allow the same volume of water [and corresponding land acreages] to feed two Americans instead of one, with no loss in overall nutrition.[64]

Vegan Action agrees. "In a time when population pressures have become an increasing stress on the environment," it says on its website,

Demonstrators protest the wasting of water on farms. Scientists and farmers agree that raising farm animals requires large amounts of water.

1 lb. of meat equals 2,463 gallons

there are additional arguments for a vegan diet. The United Nations has reported that a vegan diet can feed many more people than an animal-based diet. For instance, projections have estimated that the 1992 food supply could have fed about 6.3 billion people on a purely vegetarian diet, 4.2 billion people on an 85% vegetarian diet, or 3.2 billion people on a 75% vegetarian [and 25% meat-eating] diet.[65]

Water and Soil Pollution

Issues of water pollution and soil erosion and pollution are also directly related to wasteful uses of water. Leading vegan groups complain that animal agriculture's quest for higher yields speeds up the erosion of fertile topsoil, making the land less productive. In turn, that prompts farmers to convert more forests and other wilderness areas to farmland for crops and grazing land for various animals. In this scenario, forests all across the world are disappearing at an alarming rate.

At the same time, the animal wastes produced by farms, including large-scale factory farms that supply enormous amounts of chicken, beef, and pork, make their way into groundwater and rivers. This pollution has been detected and in some cases measured by the UN Food and Agriculture Organization (UNFAO). The UNFAO reports that animal agriculture annually injects large amounts of pesticides, manure, and fertilizers into soil, coastal ecosystems, and drinking water for towns and cities. This includes millions of gallons of liquefied feces and urine that seep from overflowing waste storage ponds. Hundreds of spills of such toxic materials have been documented, as have clouds of airborne fecal particles from such storage facilities. On many occasions, officials in towns located near large factory farms where pigs are raised have cautioned residents to wear masks while outdoors. Not surprisingly, the UN has documented that hundreds of people have become sick and millions of fish have died from such pollution.

The UN is not the only organization that has observed and reported such waste and pollution. According to the Natural Resources Defense Council, "Giant livestock farms, which can house hundreds of thousands of pigs, chickens, or cows, produce vast amounts of waste. In fact, in the U.S. these 'factory farms' generate more than 130 times the amount of waste that people do [and have] polluted more than 27,000 miles of rivers and contaminated groundwater in dozens of states."[66]

Fighting Climate Change

Animal agriculture also contributes to ongoing climate change by pumping diverse greenhouse gases into the atmosphere. This occurs in a number of ways. First, the belching and flatulence of mammals raised for meat and other body parts contain a high volume of methane, a potent greenhouse gas. Scientists estimate that as much as 16 percent of the world's annual production of methane comes from these two sources alone.

This problem has become so pressing that government leaders increasingly address it in writings and speeches. Pete Hodgson, New Zealand's minister for energy, science, and fisheries, is one of these leaders. He provides a helpful overview of the effects on the environment of such excess:

> One ton of methane, the chief agricultural greenhouse gas, has the global warming potential of 23 tons of carbon dioxide. A dairy cow produces about 75 kilograms of methane a year, equivalent to over 1.5 tons of carbon dioxide. The cow, of course, is only doing what comes naturally. But people are inclined to forget, it seems, that farming is an industry. We cleared the land, sowed the pasture, bred the stock, and so on. It's a human business, not a natural one. We're pretty good at it, which is why atmospheric concentrations of methane increased by 150 percent over the past 250 years, while carbon dioxide concentrations increased by 30 percent.[67]

The problem is that these gases cause the lower parts of the atmosphere to warm up a little at a time. That does not cause it to become warm everywhere in the world, which

is a common fallacy. (This mistaken idea spread partly because of a misinterpretation of the older name for climate change—global warming.) Rather, as the global ocean of air rises in temperature, it spawns changes in traditional weather patterns. More often than not, regions with hot summers develop even hotter summers; conversely, areas that experience cold winters may start having winters that are colder still, and with more snow than usual, too. At the same time, the oceans are expanding in volume and are already changing coastlines in unpredictable and unwanted ways. By the start of the second half of the present century, experts predict that numerous coastal cities could be flooded.

Serious vegans point out that if enough people adopted a vegan approach to eating and living, these negative effects of climate change would diminish rather than increase over

Enormous amounts of animal waste produced by large-scale factory farms that raise large numbers of chickens, cattle, and hogs end up in groundwater, creeks, and rivers.

U.S. Greenhouse Gas Emissions

A 2006 study conducted by University of Chicago geophysicists Gidon Eshel and Pamela Martin found that production of excess greenhouse gases is increased by the huge numbers of cattle and other animals raised for meat. According to Eshel, the United States is responsible for roughly 28 percent of global greenhouse gas emissions. "The U.S. has five sectors of the economy that are large emitters," he states. They are "transportation, industrial, commercial, residential, and agriculture." The researchers report that a hefty portion of the problem comes from producing foods that are energy inefficient, including cattle and the feed they consume. "I say eat whatever works for you," Eshel states, "but just keep in mind that the less animal-based food you eat, and the more you replace those calories with plant-based food, the better off you are, in terms of your health as well as your contributions to the health of the planet."

Quoted in ABC News. "Meat-Eaters Aiding Global Warming?" April 19, 2006. http://abcnews.go.com/Technology/story?id=1856817&page=1.

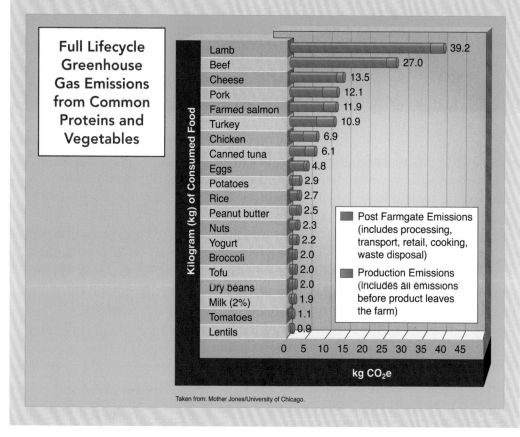

Full Lifecycle Greenhouse Gas Emissions from Common Proteins and Vegetables

Kilogram (kg) of Consumed Food

Food	kg CO$_2$e
Lamb	39.2
Beef	27.0
Cheese	13.5
Pork	12.1
Farmed salmon	11.9
Turkey	10.9
Chicken	6.9
Canned tuna	6.1
Eggs	4.8
Potatoes	2.9
Rice	2.7
Peanut butter	2.5
Nuts	2.3
Yogurt	2.2
Broccoli	2.0
Tofu	2.0
Dry beans	2.0
Milk (2%)	1.9
Tomatoes	1.1
Lentils	0.9

■ Post Farmgate Emissions (includes processing, transport, retail, cooking, waste disposal)

■ Production Emissions (Includes all emissions before product leaves the farm)

kg CO$_2$e

Taken from: Mother Jones/University of Chicago.

time. Mat McDermott, a New York City–based expert on resource consumption and animal welfare issues, explains that

> if people switched from current levels of meat consumption common in Europe and the United States to a diet based on plant-based protein, pastures would be allowed to regrow as forest. If this transition of dietary norms [had] started in 2010 and [was] completed by 2030, and that pasture and cropland was allowed to regrow as forest, it would soak up such large amounts of CO_2 that, in combination with the resultant reduction of methane emissions due to the animals themselves, the costs of [dealing with] climate change ... would drop by 70% by 2050. ... Even if large numbers of people stopped eating beef and meat from other ruminant animals and the resultant land [was] freed up to regrow as forest, or even converted to production of biofuels, then climate change ... costs would drop by 50%.[68]

Large rectangular pools hold farm animal manure on a factory hog farm in Missouri. Such pools release large amounts of methane gas into the atmosphere, contributing to global warming.

Threats to Human Health

In addition to causing water and soil pollution and hastening the onset of climate change, large-scale animal agriculture poses some very real threats to the health of both humans and wild animals. This happens partly because various fertilizers and herbicides routinely employed in such farming can poison other living things. Corn grown for animal feed is particularly susceptible. As journalist and environmental activist Michael Pollan reported in a revealing article for the *New York Times Magazine*:

> If you follow the corn [back] to the fields where it grows, you will find an 80-million-acre monoculture that consumes more chemical herbicide and fertilizer than any other crop. Keep going and you can trace the nitrogen runoff from that crop all the way down the Mississippi into the Gulf of Mexico, where it has created (if that is the right word) a 12,000-square-mile "dead zone" [in which fish and other marine life can no longer live]. But you can go farther still, and follow the fertilizer needed to grow that corn all the way to the oil fields of the Persian Gulf [where its ingredients originate]. Assuming [a steer] continues to eat 25 pounds of corn a day and reaches a weight of 1,250 pounds, he will have consumed in his lifetime roughly 284 gallons of oil. We have succeeded in industrializing the beef calf, transforming what was once a solar-powered ruminant into the very last thing we need: another fossil-fuel machine.[69]

HEALTH FACT

According to the U.S. Department of Agriculture, cooking poultry to a temperature of 165°F (74°C) kills any germs that may have made their way into the creatures due to their having been kept in crowded conditions in the factory farm system.

Another way that large-scale animal agriculture threatens the health of both people and animals is by creating new, antibiotic-resistant strains of bacteria. Cows raised for their meat, for example, are routinely given large doses of antibiotics in their feed to keep them healthy. Scientists have been warning for years that this practice stimulates the evolution of "superbugs" in the cows' intestines. In the past a majority of the bacteria that grew in bovine innards and

ended up on human plates was killed on contact with people's stomach acid. This is not the case with the new superbugs, however. "The digestive tract of the modern feedlot cow is closer in acidity to our own," Pollan writes, "and in this new, manmade environment, acid-resistant strains of *E. coli* have developed that can survive our stomach acids and go on to kill us."[70]

One way to avoid these problems, Pollan and other environmental experts say, is to take an alternate approach. It consists of eating beef and other animal meat that comes from cows that eat only grass. If that occurred, they point out, noxious fertilizers and herbicides would not get into the meat. Nor would new, dangerous strains of bacteria be created in the animals' guts. The meat would likely be more

Many environmental and nutritional experts advise meat eaters to eat beef that comes from cows who eat grass rather than corn.

expensive, these experts admit. "But would that necessarily be a bad thing?" Pollan asks.

> Eating beef every day might not be such a smart idea anyway, for our health [and] for the environment. And how cheap, really, is [today's] cheap feedlot beef? Not cheap at all, when you add in the invisible costs: antibiotic resistance, environmental degradation, heart disease, *E. coli* poisoning, corn subsidies, imported oil, and so on. All these are costs that grass-fed beef does not incur.[71]

What If Everyone Became Vegan?

Noted veganism advocate Erik Marcus tells what he thinks would happen to the planet's animals and ecology if all people suddenly became vegans.

There's no doubt that if the entire world switched overnight to a vegan diet, there would be hundreds of millions of farmed animals needing life-long housing and care. But realistically speaking, this scenario could never occur, as there's simply no possibility that the entire worldwide population would become vegan in an instant. It would be delusional to think that the world would require anything less than several decades to become entirely vegan. And if there's one thing that animal agriculture is great at, it is calibrating supply to meet demand. So if the consumption of animal products fell into steady decline, we would see fewer and fewer farmed animals being bred, and substantial tracts of land becoming available to wildlife. Over time, the world's farm animals would be displaced by countless species of wild animals. Ultimately, cows, pigs, and chickens are domesticated animals and are no more important to biodiversity than, say, toy poodles. Decades from now there may be hobbyists who breed a handful of these animals, for the sake of preserving certain breeds. But the fact is that biodiversity is harmed rather than helped by the existence of animal agriculture.

Erik Marcus. "If Everyone Became Vegan, What Would Happen to All the Animals?" Vegan.com. http://vegan.com/articles/faq/#happen%20to%20all%20the%20animals.

Thinking About the Future

Vegans go a significant step further and advocate the elimination of these flesh foods entirely. In their view if a majority of Americans adopted a vegan diet, far fewer cows, pigs, chickens, and other animals raised for meat would be bred, fattened, and slaughtered in the factory farm system. This would not only free up more water and land, they say, but also reduce environmental pollution and lessen the incidence of human illness and death from the effects of poisons and superbugs. In dedicated vegan Christina Pirello's words, pesticides, herbicides, antibiotics, and other substances that enter human food via animal feed

> are all compromising our food, contributing to the obesity epidemic, speeding up the degeneration of our health, and putting the health of the planet at risk. These scientific and technological advances are making slaves of us all. . . . The future of our food is in jeopardy, but it is also in our hands. By choosing to rethink your life and how you live it, by choosing to feed yourself in a healthy and sustainable way that creates personal health *and* planetary health, you decide what that future will look like.[72]

CHAPTER 6

Some Major Vegan Controversies

Most vegans, like most nonvegans, would like to concentrate on living their lives without arousing any undue public notice. However, a number of controversial questions and accusations about veganism do crop up from time to time in books, magazines, newspapers, radio and TV news and commentary programs, and the Internet. These touchy topics tend to spread misconceptions about veganism and negatively affect vegans' image among many nonvegans.

For example, some vegans claim that eating a vegan diet ensures good health and cures certain diseases, including cancer. Another contentious issue is whether vegans should impose their plant-based diet on their infants and small children. Still another controversy revolves around pets, as some vegans feel that owning a pet is a type of slavery. Needless to say, the numerous pet-friendly beliefs and customs ingrained in American and other Western societies hardly seem like "pet slavery" to loving pet owners. The manner in which vegans respond to and deal with such controversies may well continue to affect the way many nonvegans view veganism in the foreseeable future.

Exaggerated Health Claims

Many, if not most, vegans attest to feeling better, both physically and mentally, after converting to a vegan diet. This is to be expected, doctors and other medical authorities say. After all, in addition to meat, many nonvegans consume too many high-calorie foods containing refined flour and sugar, saturated fats, and other substances that are considered unhealthy. So someone who switches to eating only grains, nuts, vegetables, fruits, and other unarguably healthy foods will almost certainly feel better. Few, therefore, would doubt or argue with Judy's answer to an interviewer's question about whether she felt healthier since becoming a vegan. "According to my doctor," she replied, "I'm very healthy. I take no pills or medicines. I've been told I look a lot younger than my age."[73] Similarly, when asked about his health since he switched to vegan eating, Alan said, "I definitely feel better than I did when I ate meat. I often used to feel like I just didn't have enough energy to get up in the morning. Now, I have tons of energy and feel like I can't wait to get out of bed each day. Also, I feel alert most of the time and am able to

Some vegans believe that owning a pet is tantamount to enslaving the animal, a position that has spawned much controversy.

get many more things done in an average day since I became a vegan."[74]

It must be stressed that testimonials like those of Alan and other vegans who claim that their vegan diet has improved their health represent the experiences of only a select few from the vegan community, which consists of millions of individuals. Their experiences may not reflect the feelings of all, or even most, vegans.

Even more unreliable, are reports that consuming a vegan diet may cure various diseases and serious medical conditions. Gentle World, a nonprofit organization dedicated to educating people about the benefits of veganism, conducted interviews with a number of vegans through Facebook. One question asked was: "What physical conditions have miracu-

Many nonvegans consume too many high-calorie, processed foods containing refined flour and sugar, saturated fat, and other substances that are considered unhealthful to eat.

lously gone away since you became vegan?" A respondent named Sue answered:

> My asthma, which I thought would kill me by the time I was 40, disappeared completely in just a few weeks. From the constant use of two kinds of inhaler and being threatened with steroid injections I went to [being] wheeze-free and I haven't needed meds for 17 years. I also stopped having colds. I get the occasional sniffle but never anything serious. I get what I call colds but they only last 24 or 48 hours and are nothing like the ones I used to get before I went vegan.[75]

Other vegans interviewed claimed a wide range of even more astounding cures. Some said that their arthritis had disappeared, while still others reported they were no longer plagued by acne, diabetes, allergies, and a host of other afflictions. Doctors who review such claims frequently point out that the people who make them usually are not intentionally misrepresenting the truth. The question is not whether an allergy went away, but whether it was specifically the vegan diet that was responsible for its disappearance. Allergies are caused by eating or otherwise coming into contact with specific allergens (allergy-causing substances). When people become vegan, they change many aspects of their diet. If one of those changes happens to eliminate the substance that causes their particular allergy, the allergy symptoms will disappear. However, if they had eliminated that substance without becoming vegan, the symptoms would have disappeared as well.

A Cure for Cancer?

Perhaps the most questionable and controversial health claims made by vegans are those that say a vegan diet cured cancer. A debilitating and often fatal disease, cancer affects some 10 million people annually worldwide. Meanwhile, in North America one in every four people who contract cancer die from it

HEALTH FACT

Some vegans feed their pets vegan diets to match their own dietary preferences. Nutritionists say this can work for dogs, but cats require a certain amount of animal protein to remain healthy and therefore should not be put on strict vegan diets.

Vegans Take Offense

In a 2007 article in the *New York Times*, reporter Nina Planck criticized vegans who feed their babies strict plant-based diets. She said in part, "Though it's not politically correct to say so, all diets are not created equal. An adult who was well-nourished *in utero* and in infancy may choose to get by on a vegan diet, but babies are built from protein, calcium, cholesterol and fish oil. Children fed only plants will not get the precious things they need to live and grow."[1]

Numerous vegans, including several experts in nutrition, took offense and denounced what they saw as an unfair and misinformed attack. One of these experts, vegan dietitian Reed Mangels, later stated in an article posted by the Vegetarian Resource Group:

> The *New York Times* opinion piece concluded with a call to parents to raise their children as non-vegetarians and to allow them to choose their own diets as adults. I don't get the logic. Parents are choosing what foods their children eat, even if they are raising them as meat eaters. I could just as easily say that all parents should raise their children as vegans and then, if the children grow up and want to eat meat, that would be their choice. As parents, we make choices for our children, based on what we think is in their best interest.[2]

1. Nina Planck. "Death by Veganism." *New York Times*, May 21, 2007. www.nytimes.com/2007/05/21/opinion/21planck.html?_r=1&.
2. Reed Mangels. "Vegan Children: Response to *NYT* Op-ed." Vegetarian Resource Group, April 25, 2012. www.vrg.org/blog/2012/04/25/vegan-children-response-to-nyt-op-ed.

Nonvegans say that putting an infant on a vegan diet deprives the child of adequate protein, calcium, cholesterol, and fish oil, all of which a growing body needs to properly develop. Vegans disagree.

Many medical studies have shown that a vegan diet helps reduce the risk of cancer. Other studies have contradicted this, however.

each year. A great deal of research is ongoing around the globe in the search for cures; to date there is no proof that a vegan diet is a cure for cancer.

What various medical studies by reputable organizations *have* found is that a vegetarian or vegan diet is sometimes associated with a *reduced risk* of getting cancer. These groups, among them the World Cancer Research Fund and the American Institute for Cancer Research, explain that this does not mean becoming a vegan protects someone from getting cancer. The truth is that everyone—vegans and nonvegans alike—*might* get cancer. The medical authorities directing the studies say simply that, compared with a meat-eating diet, eating a meatless diet may lower the risk of getting cancer. The prestigious American Cancer Society agrees, saying, "Vegetarian diets include many healthful features. They tend to be low in saturated fats and high in fiber, vitamins, and phytochemicals. It is not possible to conclude at this time, however, that a vegetarian diet has any special benefits for the prevention of cancer."[76]

Veganism and Pregnancy

One controversy with far-reaching effects is the relationship between a vegan diet and the health of a growing human fetus. Doctors and other medical authorities are somewhat divided on this matter. Some agree with Columbia University's Drew Ramsey, who believes that a vegan diet may not be totally healthy even for a full-grown adult, much less a fragile fetus. Some physicians, including Ramsey, suggest, for instance, that the fetus's developing bones are at risk if the mother's diet contains too little calcium, a mineral found in dairy products, which vegans avoid. Ramsey expresses particular concern about brain development. "A vegan diet during pregnancy," he states, "also puts the fetal brain in danger of stunted development and reduced cognitive capacities later in life."[77]

Other doctors are less worried. They believe the growing fetus is not at risk as long as the mother gets proper nutrition herself. This is the official position of the Academy of Nutrition and Dietetics, which says, "An evidence-based review showed that vegetarian diets can be nutritionally adequate in pregnancy and result in positive maternal and infant health outcomes."[78]

The question, it appears, is how to ensure that a pregnant vegan will know what key nutrients, such as vitamin B_{12}, she needs in order to ensure her fetus's health and whether she will be responsible enough to consume the necessary

The Vegan Middle Ground on Pets

The issue of whether vegans can or should have pets is far from straightforward. There is a large gray area composed of opinions in the middle. Elaine Vigneault, who calls herself the Eccentric Vegan on her entertaining website, Vegan Soapbox, is one who takes this middle ground. She states:

> It's up to each individual, but my opinion is this. If you rescue animals, great. That's not doing harm, that's doing good. But if you buy a "pet" from a breeder or pet store, that's doing harm. That's creating a market for breeders, including puppy mills. Moreover, that's formalizing the animal's status as property, not as family member or companion. *Buying* animals, dead or alive, is not vegan.

Eccentric Vegan. "Can Vegans Have Pets?" Vegan Soapbox, November 2, 2008. www.vegansoapbox.com/can-vegans-have-pets.

nutrients on a regular basis. Well-known vegan nutrition expert Jack Norris believes that dedicated vegans can be counted on in such situations. "I rarely come across a pregnant vegan who does not know the importance of making sure she is getting vitamin B_{12},"[79] he remarks.

An article in the online health magazine *Everyday Health* takes a similar stance. It agrees that "it's extremely important to get adequate nutrition during pregnancy," but agrees with Norris and adds,

> You shouldn't assume you have to change your eating habits simply because you're expecting, as long as you're eating a well-rounded diet and taking the right supplements. These may include a prenatal vitamin, omega-3 supplement, and possibly B_{12} or folic acid (depending on how much of these are included in the prenatal vitamin). Pregnant vegans should talk about their diet with their healthcare provider and possibly also consult a nutritionist who specializes in prenatal nutrition to make sure they're getting all the nourishment they and their baby need.[80]

Feeding Newborns

A related, no less controversial issue deals with whether an infant who is born healthy can eat a vegan diet and *remain* healthy. Some parents who are strict vegans have insisted on feeding their newborns the same foods they consume. There is no way to know how many babies have suffered from various degrees of malnutrition as a result. But news reports and court cases confirm that a few such infants have died of that condition because their parents put them on a vegan diet. One of the more recent cases occurred in 2007 in Atlanta, Georgia. Six-week-old Crown Shakur died of malnutrition at a body weight of 3.5 pounds (1.6kg) after existing mainly on soy milk and apple juice. The child's parents were convicted of murder, involuntary manslaughter, and cruelty.

As in the case of vegans and pregnancy, opinions differ widely on this issue. Some people—mostly nonvegans, including some doctors—feel that it is too risky to give a new baby a strict vegan diet. They worry that a few key nutrients—especially folic acid, vitamin B_{12}, protein, and calcium—may not be present in sufficient quantities in the child's food. As a result, the infant may suffer from serious deficiencies of such nutrients. Many vegans agree with this view. This is shown by the fact that most vegan mothers breast-feed their infants rather than feed them vegan foods. "I think parents should feed their baby a healthy diet," vegan mother Arlene said in an interview. Such a healthy diet, she believes, can be provided by breast-feeding, "which provides all the nutrients a baby needs."[81]

A growing number of respected medical authorities have reviewed the issue of whether vegan parents can feed their newborns a plant-based diet. The overall consensus of these physicians is infants *can* eat plant-based foods as long as their parents are extremely careful and have discussed all aspects of that diet beforehand with a doctor or licensed nutritionist. The approach in such cases is to be on the safe side and supplement the diet's regular vegan foods with extra vitamins, protein, calcium, and other nutrients as necessary. An article for the online version of the Learning Channel provides a well-worded, brief overview of this growing opinion in the medical community. "When parents raise infants

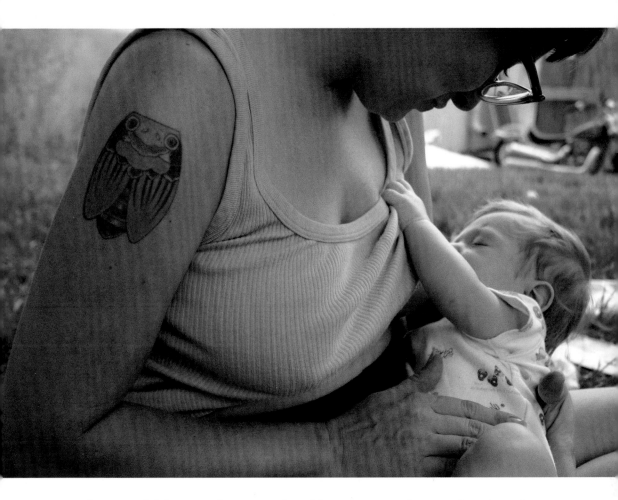

and young children on alternative diets like veganism, there is no room for error," it cautions.

A well-planned and carefully executed vegan diet can, however, adequately support children. Most vegan mothers nurse their infants. Breast milk enhances the immune system, lowers the child's risk of infection, and helps prevent allergies. Breastfeeding vegan mothers [should] take supplements to compensate for their vitamin D and B_{12} deficiencies. When breastfeeding is impossible, vegan formulas offer an alternative. As a rule, experts agree that homemade formula or nondairy milks do not meet a baby's nutritional needs. Older vegan babies and toddlers can eat pureed fruits and vegetables, mashed tofu, soy yogurt and fortified soy, rice or oat milks.[82]

Some say that vegan mothers who breast-feed their babies should take supplements to compensate for inadequate levels of vitamins D and B_{12} in their diet.

The Issue of Having Pets

Without doubt, few vegan-related issues are liable to start a heated argument faster than the question of pet ownership. Some of the strictest vegans believe that having a pet in one's home is wrong. In this view, the animal is imprisoned against its will, and furthermore, owning a pet is just as wrong as owning another human being.

The United States is considered an extremely pet-friendly nation; tens of millions of households include dogs, cats, birds, hamsters, and other animal companions. As a result, most Americans consider the strict vegan belief that owning pets is unethical as far too extreme. As a matter of fact, vegan author Joanne Stepaniak, who freely admits that she is quite strict on most vegan issues, supports a more moderate view in this case. "It is irresponsible," she says,

> for people to disregard the cries of homeless or abandoned animals. A compassionate perspective calls for aiding them in whatever way we can. For some vegans this means actively striving to close breeding mills and the pet stores that support them. For others, it means contributing to no-kill shelters through donations of money or food, or volunteering to walk dogs, clean cages, and spend time playing with and giving attention to the animals. Many grassroots animal activists have, or would be interested in starting, a local spay and neuter program, which would be coordinated with city government or animal control agencies. And of course, there is always the option of adopting a companion animal in need.[83]

Cheri agrees. "We have had several dogs, all of which are/were very much part of the family," she says. They were

> never caged for the day in a pen in the yard, [but were] always treated with respect and regard for what they contribute to the family system, which is a source of unconditional love. I think it is sad there are those who believe they need to be "masters" over their pet, having them so trained that the spirit of the animal is lost. The relationship of a pet/family is hopefully

like that of human to human, in that it is based on a respect of each other's needs and desire to share [life] with another soul while here on this earth.[84]

To Their Credit

No one can read this passage and not sense the author's palpable feelings of concern and compassion. Indeed, whether dedicated vegans address owning a pet, alleviating animal suffering, cleaning up the environment, or other issues they commonly worry about, that compassion bubbles to the surface. Whether one sees them as terribly misguided or full of wisdom on a given issue, they consistently believe they are doing the right thing. That is one reason why they often sound quite optimistic about their eating choices and the possible outcomes of those choices. A good example of that optimism and sense of confidence is a series of questions that Christina Pirello poses to her readers—queries that even many meat eaters would have trouble answering with a no. "Don't you want to feel better?" she begins. "Don't you want to enjoy delicious food and know that it is really nourishing you? . . . Don't you want to leave a lighter footprint on the planet? Don't you want to live with compassion? Don't you want the world to be a better place for you having been here?"[85]

Introduction: A Decidedly Nonvegan World

1. Karen. Interview with the author, December 27, 2012.
2. American Vegan Society. "What Is Vegan?" www.americanvegan.org /vegan.htm.
3. EthicalPlanet.com. "Eating Out as a Vegan." www.ethicalplanet.com /eating-out.
4. Erik Marcus. *The Ultimate Vegan Guide: Compassionate Living Without Sacrifice*. Lexington, KY: Vegan .com, 2011, pp. 145, 153.
5. Brenda Davis and Vesanto Melina. *Becoming Vegan: The Complete Guide to Adopting a Healthy Plant-Based Diet*. Summertown, TN: Book Publishing, 2000, pp. 12–13.

Chapter 1: Veganism Through the Ages

6. Quoted in Buddhist Publication Society. "The Edicts of King Asho-ka." Translated by V.S. Dhammika. www.cs.colostate.edu/~malaiya /ashoka.html.
7. Quoted in Buddhist Publication Society. "The Edicts of King Asho-ka."
8. Quoted in Buddhist Publication Society. "The Edicts of King Asho-ka."
9. Quoted in Philip Wheelwright, ed. *The Presocratics*. New York: Macmillan, 1966, p. 222.
10. Plutarch. "On the Eating of Flesh." In *Moralia*, translated by Frank C. Babbit. Cambridge, MA: Harvard University Press, 1957, pp. 547, 551.
11. Porphyry. *On Abstinence from Animal Food*. Thrice Holy. http:// thriceholy.net/Texts/Porphyry .html.
12. Quoted in John Davis. *World Veganism: Past, Present, and Future*. International Vegetarian Union. www.ivu.org/history/Vegan_His tory.pdf.
13. Quoted in Sophia Gubb. "Leonardo da Vinci Was a Vegan." *Sophia Gubb's Blog*, September 9, 2011. www.sophiagubb.com/leonardo -da-vinci-was-a-vegan.
14. Leo Tolstoy. "The First Step." International Vegetarian Union. www .ivu.org/history/tolstoy/the_%20 first_step.html.
15. Tolstoy. "The First Step."
16. Chris Grezo. "Veganism's Journey into Mainstream and the History

of Moral Progress." Vegan Woman, August 12, 2012. www.thevegan woman.com/veganisms-journey -into-mainstream-and-the-history -of-moral-progress.

Chapter 2: Adopting a Vegan Diet and Lifestyle

17. Vegetarian Resource Group. "Veganism in a Nutshell." www.vrg.org/ nutshell/vegan.htm#books.
18. Alan. Interview with the author, January 3, 2013.
19. Joanne Stepaniak. *Being Vegan: Living with Conscience, Conviction, and Compassion.* Los Angeles: Lowell House, 2000, p. 5.
20. Gary L. Francione. "Some Thoughts on the Meaning of Vegan." *Animal Rights: The Abolitionist Approach* (blog), October 18, 2009. www .abolitionistapproach.com/some -thoughts-on-the-meaning-of-veg an/#.UQlC2Gc3nKo.
21. Susan. Interview with the author, December 21, 2012.
22. Cheri. Interview with the author, January 21, 2013.
23. Judy. Interview with the author, January 12, 2013.
24. Judy. Interview.
25. Cheri. Interview.
26. Francione, "Some Thoughts on the Meaning of Vegan."
27. Arlene. Interview with the author, January 12, 2013.
28. Christina Pirello. *This Crazy Vegan Life: A Prescription for an Endangered Species.* New York: Penguin, 2008, p. 106.
29. Pirello, *This Crazy Vegan Life*, p. 106.
30. Quoted in Vegan Action. "Frequently Asked Questions." http:// vegan.org/frequently-asked-ques tions.
31. Terry Hope Romero. *Vegan Eats World. Boston*: Da Capo, 2013, p. xvii.

Chapter 3: Vegan Nutrition and Health

32. Marcus. *The Ultimate Vegan Guide*, p. 43.
33. Marcus. *The Ultimate Vegan Guide*, p. 7.
34. Marcus. *The Ultimate Vegan Guide*, p. 43.
35. Nina Rubin. "Beyond Milk and Honey: The Vegan Controversy." *StarChefs.com*, September 2005. www.starchefs.com/cook/features /veganism-health-debate.
36. Christopher Wanjek. "Sorry, Vegans: Eating Meat and Cooking Food Made Us Human." NBCNews.com, November 19, 2012. www.nbcnews.com/id/49888012 /ns/technology_and_science-sci ence/#.UQ0vUGc3nKp.
37. Brian Patton. "We Are Not Grizzly Bears." *New York Times*, April 17, 2012. www.nytimes.com/room fordebate/2012/04/17/is-veganism -good-for-everyone/we-are-not -grizzly-bears.
38. Stepaniak. *Being Vegan*, p. 23.
39. Academy of Nutrition and Dietetics. "Vegetarian Diets." www.eat right.org/about/content.aspx?id =8357.

40. Drew Ramsey. "Meat Is Brain Food." *New York Times*, August 17, 2012. www.nytimes.com/room fordebate/2012/04/17/is-veganism -good-for-everyone/meat-is-brain -food.
41. Judy. Interview.
42. Cheri. Interview.
43. Alan. Interview.
44. Cheri. Interview.
45. Quoted in Gentle World. "Reward-ed for Being Vegan." http://gentle world.org/rewarded-for-being -vegan.
46. Quoted in Gentle World. "Reward-ed for Being Vegan."
47. Quoted in Gentle World. "Reward-ed for Being Vegan."

Chapter 4: Ideas Behind Ethical Veganism

48. Quoted in *Veganism Is Nonviolence* (blog), October 21, 2013. http:// veganismisnonviolence.com.
49. Quoted in *Veganism Is Nonviolence*.
50. Vegan Outreach. "Factory Farms." www.veganoutreach.org/whyveg an/animals.html.
51. Quoted in McDonald's Cruelty: The Rotten Truth About Egg McMuf-fins. "Experts." www.mcdonalds cruelty.com/experts.php.
52. Quoted in McDonald's Cruelty. "Experts."
53. Quoted in McDonald's Cruelty. "Experts."
54. Erik Marcus. "Prevention of Animal Suffering." Veganism.com. http:// vegan.com/articles/faq/#happen% 20to%20all%20the%20animals.

55. Vegan Society. "It's Compassionate." www.vegansociety.com/become-a -vegan/why.aspx.
56. Quoted in *UVE Archives* (blog). "Creative, Non-violent Vegan Advo-cacy (a Beginner's Guide)." February 25, 2012. http://uvearchives.word press.com.
57. Trisha Roberts. "About This Page." *Veganism Is Nonviolence* (blog). http://veganismisnonviolence.com /about-this-page.
58. Arlene. Interview.
59. Cheri. Interview.
60. Quoted in Animal Rights Zone. "Transcript of Dan Cudahy's Live Chat on 13 and 14 March 2010," March 14, 2010. http://arzone.ning .com/profiles/blogs/transcript-of -dan-cudahys-live.

Chapter 5: Vegans and the Environment

61. Worldwatch Institute. "Is Meat Sus-tainable?" www.worldwatch.org /node/549.
62. Erik Marcus. "Environmen-tal Advantages." Veganism.com. http://vegan.com/articles/faq /#happen%20to%20all%20the%20 animals.
63. Vegan Action. "For the Environ-ment." http://vegan.org/for-the -environment.
64. Vegan Outreach. "Resources and Contamination." www.veganout reach.org/whyvegan/resources .html.
65. Vegan Action. "For the Environ-ment."

66. Quoted in Worldwatch Institute. "Is Meat Sustainable?"

67. Quoted in Erik Marcus. "Environmental Advantages."

68. Mat McDermott. "Vegetarian Diet Could Cut Climate Change Mitigation Costs by 70%." TreeHugger, March 13, 2009. www.treehugger .com/green-food/vegetarian-diet -could-cut-climate-change-mitiga tion-costs-by-70.html.

69. Michael Pollan. "Power Steer." *New York Times Magazine*, March 31, 2002. wwww.nytimes.com/2002 /03/31/magazine/power-steer.html ?src=pm.

70. Pollan. "Power Steer."

71. Pollan. "Power Steer."

72. Pirello. *This Crazy Vegan Life*, pp. 7, 15.

Chapter 6: Some Major Vegan Controversies

73. Judy. Interview.

74. Alan. Interview.

75. Quoted in Gentle World. "Rewarded for Being Vegan."

76. American Cancer Society. "American Cancer Society Guidelines on Nutrition and Physical Activity for Cancer Prevention." www.cancer .org/healthy/eathealthygetactive /acsguidelinesonnutritionphysi calactivityforcancerprevention /acs-guidelines-on-nutrition-and -physical-activity-for-cancer-pre vention-diet-cancer-questions.

77. Drew Ramsey. "Meat Is Brain Food."

78. Academy of Nutrition and Dietetics. "Vegetarian Diets."

79. Jack Norris. "Vitamin B_{12} in Pregnancy." *JackNorrisRD* (blog), March 2, 2009. http://jacknorrisrd .com/?cat=8.

80. Annie Hauser. "Myth: Pregnant Women Shouldn't Be Vegan." EverydayHealth.com. www.every dayhealth.com/diet-and-nutrition -pictures/vegan-myths-debunked .aspx#/slide-6.

81. Arlene. Interview.

82. Sarah Dowdey. "Controversial Veganism." Learning Channel. http://recipes.howstuffworks.com/ vegan2.htm.

83. Stepaniak. *Being Vegan*, p. 38.

84. Cheri. Interview.

85. Pirello. *This Crazy Vegan Life*, p. xiv.

acculturate: To impart beliefs and other aspects of a given culture and society to someone.

carcinogen: A cancer-causing substance.

E. coli: A type of bacterium found in mammals' intestines. Some strains are harmless, but others cause food poisoning.

herbicide: A chemical used to destroy unwanted plants.

herbivore: A person or animal who eats a plant-based diet.

heterosexism: A bias *for* opposite-sex sexuality and relationships, with a corresponding bias *against* same-sex sexuality and relationships.

legume: A fruit-like food that grows from a pod, including peas, lentils, and beans.

miso: A traditional Japanese seasoning.

omnivore: A person or animal who eats both meat and plant foods.

paradigm: A clear example, model, or archetype for something else.

phytochemicals: Chemical compounds that occur naturally in plants.

ruminant: A mammal that digests plant-based food by chewing it, swallowing it, regurgitating it, and then chewing the half-digested food again.

sentient: A term that describes beings who can think, feel pain and loss, and feel and exhibit love and loyalty.

speciesism: A major disregard for and willingness to exploit nonhuman species.

supplements: Concentrated ingredients in vitamin form to make up for any dietary deficiency.

American Vegan Society (AVS)

56 Dinshah Ln., PO Box 369
Malaga, NJ 08328
(856) 694-2887
fax: (856) 694-2288
www.americanvegan.org

The AVS is a nonprofit educational membership organization that teaches a compassionate way of living that includes veganism. According to its mission, it strives to teach humans to revere the earth, save the animals, and care for themselves.

Boston Vegetarian Society (BVS)

PO Box 38-1071
Cambridge, MA 02238-1071
(617) 424-8846
www.bostonveg.org

The BVS provides a community for vegetarians, vegans, and anyone wanting to learn more about the benefits of plant-based eating and the impact of food choices on animals, the environment, and personal health. It sponsors educational seminars, vegan cooking classes, and outreach events.

Christian Vegetarian Association (CVA)

PO Box 201791
Cleveland, OH 44120
(216) 283-6702
fax: (216) 283-6702
www.all-creatures.org/cva

The CVA promotes healthy, Christ-centered and God-honoring living among Christians by advocating nutritious plant-based diets in the global Christian community.

EarthSave International

20555 Devonshire St., Ste. 105
Chatsworth, CA 91311
(415) 234-0829
fax: (818) 337-1957
www.earthsave.org

EarthSave International helps people make food choices that promote health, reduce health-care costs, and provide greater health independence.

Vegan Outreach

PO Box 30865
Tucson, AZ 85751-0865
(520) 495-0503
fax: (520) 495-0503
www.veganoutreach.org

Vegan Outreach is a nonprofit organization that works to expose and end cruelty to animals through the widespread distribution of its illustrated booklets.

A Well-Fed World

815 Otis Pl. NW
Washington, DC 20010
(202) 495-1348
fax: (347) 710-7065
http://awellfedworld.org

This hunger-relief and animal-protection organization promotes the benefits of sustainable, plant-centered solutions in response to global food security, health, hunger, and environmental concerns.

Worldwatch Institute

1400 Sixteenth St. NW, Ste. 430
Washington, DC 20036
(202) 745-8092
fax: (202) 478-2534
www.worldwatch.org

The Worldwatch Institute works to accelerate the transition to a sustainable world in which the environment can be kept safe and viable to meet human needs.

FOR MORE INFORMATION

Books

Matt Ball and Bruce Friedrich. *The Animal Activist's Handbook*. New York: Lantern, 2009. The authors make a strongly worded argument that the world would be a much better place if people stopped exploiting animals for food and adopted vegan diets.

Beverly L. Bennett and Ray Sammartano. *The Complete Idiot's Guide to Vegan Living*. New York: Alpha, 2012. This book contains a wealth of information about veganism, including its history, the motives for becoming vegan, dietary and health facts, and much more.

Kris Carr. *Crazy, Sexy Diet*. Guilford, CT: Skirt!, 2001. Carr provides a great deal of information about vegan diets and how to get the most nutrition from them.

Tovar Cerulli. *The Mindful Carnivore: A Vegetarian's Hunt for Sustenance*. New York: Pegasus, 2012. In this thoughtfully written book, a former vegan and avid hunter offers possible ways that vegans and meat eaters might reach certain compromises and maintain close ties to nature in the process.

Kathy Divine. *Vegans Are Cool*. Fremantle, Western Australia: Vivid, 2011. A collection of essays written by vegans from around the world, explaining why they choose to be vegans and how veganism can change the world for the better.

Erik Marcus. *The Ultimate Vegan Guide: Compassionate Living Without Sacrifice*. Lexington, KY: Vegan.com, 2011. This well-researched, well-written volume covers almost all of the major vegan issues, including the ethical and environmental ones.

John McCabe. *Extinction: The Death of Waterlife on Planet Earth*. London: Carmania, 2011. McCabe argues that, according to science, human farming, hunting, and food production practices are depleting the oceans of life and that adopting veganism might help save the planet.

Jack Norris and Virginia Messina. *Vegan for Life: Everything You Need to Know to Be Healthy and Fit on a Plant-Based Diet*. New York: Da Capo, 2011. A detailed, authoritative explanation of proper vegan nutrition.

Christina Pirello. *This Crazy Vegan Life: A Prescription for an Endangered Species*. New York: Penguin, 2008. The author, an Emmy-winning TV chef, explains why she thinks that becoming vegan increases health and makes people better citizens.

Terry Hope Romero. *Vegan Eats World.* New York: Da Capo, 2013. A comprehensive vegan cookbook, along with some comments about veganism itself.

Ruby Roth. *Vegan Is Love: Having Heart and Taking Action.* Berkeley, CA: North Atlantic, 2012. The author effectively introduces the basics of a vegan diet and lifestyle to younger readers in this beautifully illustrated volume.

Lars Thomsen and Reuben Proctor. *Veganissimo A to Z: A Comprehensive Guide to Identifying and Avoiding Ingredients of Animal Origin in Everyday Products.* New York: Experiment, 2013. In easy-to-read prose, the authors show how animal products have made their way into not only food, but also cosmetics, photography, clothing, cleaning products, musical instruments, electronics, and more, and how adopting veganism might help reverse this process.

Bob Torres and Jenna Torres. *Being Vegan in a Non-vegan World.* Oakland, CA: PM, 2010. The authors discuss practical ways for people to make the change from a standard diet to a vegan one and how to deal with social pressures that label veganism as a weird cult.

Websites

In Defense of Animals (www.idausa .org). The website of this advocacy group centered in San Rafael, California, offers information about how people can help stop cruelty to and unnecessary killing of animals around the world.

Raptitude (www.raptitude.com). This blog provides the recollections of a person who, after trying veganism, decided to continue indefinitely. This site is extremely valuable because it contains hundreds of short but very revealing letters from vegans and non-vegans alike, who provide opinions on the author's experiences.

Veganism in a Nutshell, Vegetarian Resource Group (www.vrg.org/nut shell/vegan.htm#books). Members of the nonprofit Vegetarian Resource Group provide this straightforward basic guide to becoming vegan.

Vegan 2000: Lifestyle of the Millennium (http://library.thinkquest.org /C004833/default_en.shtml). One of the leading online groups promoting veganism provides arguments to support the notion that it is spiritually uplifting to adopt a vegan diet and lifestyle. The website also contains an eye-opening list of well-known vegans throughout history.

INDEX

A

Academy of Nutrition and Dietetics, 39, 45, 84

Activism, by vegans, 9–10

philosophy behind, 51–52

Agriculture

  animal, climate change and, 70–71

  development of, 11–12

  See also Factory farm system

Agriculture and Consumer Protection Department of the United Nations, 66

American Cancer Society, 84

American Journal of Clinical Nutrition, 42

American Vegan Society, 7

Animal products, decisions to reject, 30–31

Antibiotic-resistant bacteria, 74–75

Aquinas, Thomas (saint), 18

Ashoka (Asoka, Buddhist king), 12–13, *13*

Augustine (saint), 18

B

Bacteria, antibiotic-resistant, 74–75

Battery cages, *57,* 58

Breastfeeding, 87

British Vegan Society, 22

British Vegetarian Society, 22

Brown, Lester, *66*

Buddhism, 12, 14

C

Calcium, 45

  dietary sources of, *47, 48*

Cancer, claims of vegan diet curing, 81, 83–84

Chickens

  safe cooking of, 74

  treatment of, in factory farms, 56, 58, 67

Climate change, 70–71

Clinton, Bill, 22

Clinton, Chelsea, 22

Corn, grown for animal feed, 74

Cows, *63, 75*

  annual methane production by, 70

  grass-fed, benefits of, 75–76

Crops, animals killed in production of, 53, 63

Cudahy, Dan, 54–55, 59–60, 62, 64

D

Da Vinci, Leonardo, *19,* 19–20

Davis, Brenda, 10

Department of Agriculture, US, 74

Digestive system, *43*

Dinshah, H. Jay, 22

E

The Enlightenment, 20–21

EthicalPlanet.com (website), 9

Vegan diet
    can feed more people tan meat-based
        diets, 69
    health claims regarding, 78, 79–81
    for infants, 82, 86–87
    nutritional shortfalls in, 43, 45–46
    for pets, 81
    in pregnancy, 84–85
    variety of, 32–35
Vegan Eats World (Romero), 36
Vegan Society, 58
Veganism
    definition of, 7, 25–27
    gradual adoption of, 33
    prevalence of, 7–8
Veganism Is Nonviolence (web blog), 61
Vegetarian Resource Group (VRG), 24,
    34, 47–48
Vegetarianism, early promoters of,
    20–21
Vitamin B_{12}, 45
    deficiency in, 45–46

dietary sources of, 48
    recommended dosage of, 84
Vitamin D, 45, 49
VRG (Vegetarian Resource Group), 24,
    34, 47–48

W

Water
    pollution of, from animal agriculture,
        69–70
    use in animal agriculture, 67–68
*Water and Vegetable Diet in Consumption,
    Scrofula, Cancer, Asthma, and Other
    Chronic Diseases* (Lambe), 20
Wheldon, Rupert H., 14
World Vegan Day, 22
Worldwatch Institute, 65

Z

Zinc, 45
    dietary sources of, 48, *49*

PICTURE CREDITS

ABOUT THE AUTHOR

In addition to his numerous acclaimed volumes on ancient civilizations, historian Don Nardo has published several studies of modern scientific and medical discoveries and phenomena. Among these are *Germs, Atoms, Biological Warfare, Eating Disorders, Breast Cancer, Vaccines, Malnutrition, DNA Forensics, Sleep Disorders,* and biographies of scientists Charles Darwin and Tycho Brahe. Nardo, who also composes orchestral music, lives with his wife, Christine, in Massachusetts.